By gloriously weaving the new covenant into the study of this Exodus passage, Steve Smallman compellingly and comprehensively reveals the God of love and grace pursuing us, redeeming us, and making a way to know him and enjoy his presence through the atoning work of the cross. I have easily adapted this as a study guide for small groups in a forty day, semester, or yearlong format. Participants have found themselves invited into an experience with God so foundational to solid discipleship that it has spread to friends in other churches who are now using it as well.

—**Libby Cannizzaro**, Former Women's Ministry Coordinator, The Falls Church (Anglican)

In a hurried and cacophonous world, Steve's gentle and wise insights, farmed by Scripture reading, hymns, and prayers, will help readers grow in the knowledge of God, pointing in every meditation from Moses and his experience on the mountain to the Lord Jesus Christ.

—**Michael Kelly**, Assistant Professor of Old Testament, Westminster Theological Seminary

Steve Smallman invites us in these daily devotions to follow Moses in his passion to press on to know the presence of God. I was greatly blessed by Steve's challenge.

—**Rose Marie Miller**, Author, *From Fear to Freedom*

Steve Smallman is an experienced, godly pastor with a heart for helping people grow in the knowledge of God—not just theologically but also experientially. The scriptural meditations will refresh your spirit, renew your passion for God, and help you to find rest in the gospel grace of Jesus Christ.

—**Philip Graham Ryken**, President, Wheaton College

This book is just what one expects from a seasoned pastor who has a heart for providing edifying nourishment for the soul. What is particularly refreshing is a view of God's grace often overlooked in God's dealing with Moses on the mountain.

    —**Robert I. Vasholz**, Author, *The Old Testament Canon in the Old Testament Church*

As usual, Steve Smallman leads us to Christ. As we follow Steve's lead, we discover that Christ is leading us to himself. Follow along for forty days and see his glory.

    —**John Yenchko**, Pastor, North Shore Community Church, Oyster Bay, New York

Forty Days
on the
Mountain

FORTY DAYS
ON THE
MOUNTAIN

Meditations on
Knowing God

STEPHEN
SMALLMAN

P&R PUBLISHING

P.O. BOX 817 • PHILLIPSBURG • NEW JERSEY 08865-0817

Previously issued 2007 by Crossway Books
Reissued 2016 by P&R Publishing

Printed in the United States of America

Library of Congress Cataloging-in-Publication Data

Smallman, Stephen, 1940-
Forty days on the mountain : meditations on knowing God / Stephen Smallman.
   pages cm
ISBN 978-1-62995-116-4 (pbk.) -- ISBN 978-1-62995-117-1 (epub) -- ISBN 978-1-62995-118-8 (mobi)
   1. Moses (Biblical leader). 2. God (Christianity)--Knowableness. 3. Spiritual life--Christianity. 4. Spiritual exercises. I. Title.
BS580.M6S495 2016
242'.2--dc23

                                        2015033585

To the congregation of McLean Presbyterian Church,
which it was my joy and privilege to serve from 1967 to 1996.
As Paul wrote to the Philippian congregation:
"I thank my God in all my remembrance of you."

Contents

Contents

Acknowledgments

As I explain in the Introduction, *Forty Days on the Mountain* began several years ago as a personal journal that I wrote while on a sabbatical from McLean Presbyterian Church. I appreciate the people along the way who have continued to encourage me to get it published. Among them are: Dick Strong, who passed manuscript copies along to numbers of people he ministered to; Libby Cannizzaro, who has used it as a tool to disciple dozens of Young Life leaders; Betty Herron, who found it a great comfort during her last months on this earth; and most persistent of all, my wife, Sandy, who has encouraged me in all my writing projects but felt this was the most helpful of them all.

These meditations were originally published by Crossway Books in 2007. I appreciate the fact that the editors of P&R Publishing felt it was important to keep them in print. I have enjoyed working with Julia Craig in preparing this new edition, which is essentially unchanged from the original.

Such a book is only possible because God Almighty himself chose to make it possible that we could actually know him. May he receive all the glory if this effort can be used to help us grow in that knowledge.

Introduction

I invite you to join me as I try to capture something of what it means to know God. How can mortals like you or me—self-centered, sinful ones at that—actually think about knowing the eternal, immortal God? But that is what Moses, Paul, and countless others have desired and prayed for, and it is an opportunity that is available to us as well. In fact, that is how Jesus defined eternal life: "that they *know you* the only true God, and Jesus Christ whom you have sent" (John 17:3).

The meditations on knowing God that you are about to read grew out of a very needy time in my life. After almost twenty-five years of pastoring the same congregation (McLean Presbyterian Church, a church in suburban Washington, DC), I was granted an extended sabbatical. My wife, Sandy, and I, along with our youngest child, Andrew, went to a home near Denver, Colorado, for six months of rest and reflection. I reasoned that while a change of location and situation might provide physical rest, only the Lord could bring the deeper kind of rest I needed. And I was asking him to give it. To help accomplish this desire, I was drawn to Exodus 32–34, the remarkable passage recording Moses' meeting with God to intercede for the people of Israel. At the core of his dealings with God was a passion to know him, to know his presence, and even to be shown the glory of God.

Shortly after our arrival, I set apart one day each week to go to the library of Denver Theological Seminary to explore my chosen text through the various commentaries available to me. As you will see, door after door of understanding opened as I tried to enter vicariously into Moses' experience with God. It also took me all over the Scripture. I began writing down the insights I was gaining as journal entries just for my own benefit. Gradually I became convinced that I needed to find a way that would allow others to share in the blessing of what I was learning. Moses was on the mountain for forty days on two separate occasions. Since the unit of forty is very common in Scripture, I decided to divide up my thoughts in a format that would help others meditate on the knowledge of God for that same basic period of time. That is how *Forty Days on the Mountain* was born.

When I returned to the McLean congregation I felt renewed personally and had a new heart for the ministry.[1] Several of our members read through the manuscript of *Forty Days* and offered many helpful suggestions. They also expressed enthusiasm for what they learned. We reproduced it for limited distribution as part of our Fiftieth Anniversary Jubilee celebration. In the time since then I have returned to the themes of *Forty Days* over and over in retreats and conferences. I never fail to find that my own heart is stirred and renewed along with those who attend.

Who Should Read This Book?

These meditations are written for anyone who is serious about

---

1. Read about the remarkable confirmation of God's hand when I returned from the sabbatical, in "Kathy's Story," chap. 1 of my book *Beginnings: Understanding How We Experience the New Birth* (Phillipsburg, NJ: P&R, 2015).

knowing God. Individuals very new to the faith as well as those who are advanced in their knowledge have used *Forty Days*. It has been read by couples for their devotions, and it has been studied in small groups as the basis for training in spiritual leadership. The one thing all have in common is a sincere desire to know God.

Some of you reading this book might consider yourselves *seekers* rather than *believers*. I hope you will find this book life changing. But you need to recognize that I have two basic assumptions in writing: (1) We can know God only because God wants us to know him. "He is there and he is not silent."[2] He has made himself known through written Scripture, demonstrating this revelation by commanding Moses to write what he was told in a book.[3] (2) Knowing God ultimately comes as a result of God making himself known through his final Word—God revealed in human flesh. Authentic spirituality is anchored in the Son of God, Jesus Christ. I'm not going to try to *prove* either of these ideas—but even if you have unanswered questions (and who doesn't?) I pray that you will nevertheless patiently work through these lessons and let their truth and reality bear witness to your own heart.

How Should You Use This Book?

Obviously, there is any number of settings where these meditations would be profitable for you as an individual or for a couple or a group. But there are three expectations in my mind for those who want to gain maximum benefit from reading and studying them.

2. A phrase coined by Francis Schaeffer, who wrote a book by the same title, *He Is There and He Is Not Silent* (Wheaton, IL: Tyndale, 1972).

3. I use the masculine pronoun to refer to God without apology because the Scriptures use it for God. This is not to insist that God is male but simply that our language is limited and that this is how God has chosen to reveal himself.

The First Expectation: The Use of Scripture

It is my assumption that *Forty Days* will be read with an open Bible. I am including a portion of the text in the *English Standard Version* of the Bible at the beginning of each meditation as well as when I quote Scripture in the meditation. You will find the meditations even more profitable if you read from the Bible you ordinarily use in reading and study. That means not only using your Bible for the reading for the day, which is given at the beginning of the meditation, but keeping it open before you as you work through my remarks. My objective is that you will try to understand the teaching of the passage before making an application.

Scripture itself is the key. Let the Spirit minister to you through the Scripture with my thoughts provoking you to think about things you might not have noticed before. I hope you will find yourself going back to reread parts of the passage or even reading other places in the Bible.

As we shall see, even at the moment when God met Moses on the mountain in answer to his bold praying, what Moses received was not an experience or a vision, but a *word*. He was then told to write these words for the benefit of the people (Ex. 34:27). The written Scripture must be central if we are to enter into genuine spirituality.

The Second Expectation: The Use of Time

You need to be willing to give these readings and meditations time to sink in. I have tried to make each meditation fairly brief. But this was not done with the intention of a casual thought-for-the-day. Rather I have tried to walk deliberately through a very profound topic—the knowledge of God—one small step at a time. Don't be impatient; try to allow each day's lesson to sink in. Some have told me one meditation every day is too fast. There is certainly no requirement that these be read in forty consecutive days. But they will be more helpful if read in sequence and close enough together so that one day will prepare you for the next. I strongly encourage you to find a regular time in your day or week when you can have at least thirty minutes of quiet.

Time also allows you to stop and pray through what you have read and thought about. The entire passage is about Moses' meeting with God—which is the essence of prayer—and every day should end with a time of prayer and reflection. It will also be helpful to make use of a journal to record your own thoughts and prayers. Journal keeping is a time-honored aid to spiritual growth, and for very good reasons.

The Third Expectation: The Use of Place

For maximum benefit, I want to add a comment about the importance of place. This is, in fact, the subject of a meditation (Day 12). But several readers have encouraged me to include in my introductory words the value of locating a place (a room, a corner, a particular chair) that will serve physically as your "prayer closet." We are such harried people, and we should make use of any little thing that can aid in bringing quiet to our souls, so it is vital to have a "quiet place."

I wish I could tell you that as a result of writing these meditations I have entered fully into the knowledge of God for which I pray. But that awaits a better world. Growing up spiritually is a slow process, and I am thankful that I have been able to take a few more steps as a result of the work of preparing *Forty Days*. It is my prayer that your time with this little book and *The Book* will help you do the same.

Stephen Smallman
www.birthlineministries.com

Selections from Exodus 32–34

Exodus 32:30–35; 33:1–23; 34:1–10, 27–35

The next day Moses said to the people, "You have sinned a great sin. And now I will go up to the LORD; perhaps I can make atonement for your sin." So Moses returned to the LORD and said, "Alas, this people has sinned a great sin. They have made for themselves gods of gold. But now, if you will forgive their sin—but if not, please blot me out of your book that you have written." But the LORD said to Moses, "Whoever has sinned against me, I will blot out of my book. But now go, lead the people to the place about which I have spoken to you; behold, my angel shall go before you. Nevertheless, in the day when I visit, I will visit their sin upon them."

Then the LORD sent a plague on the people, because they made the calf, the one that Aaron made.

The LORD said to Moses, "Depart; go up from here, you and the people whom you have brought up out of the land of Egypt, to the land of which I swore to Abraham, Isaac, and Jacob, saying, 'To your offspring I will give it.' I will send an angel before you, and I will drive out the Canaanites, the Amorites, the Hittites, the Perizzites, the Hivites, and the Jebusites. Go up to a land flowing with milk and honey; but I will not go up among you, lest I consume you on the way, for you are a stiff-necked people."

When the people heard this disastrous word, they mourned, and no one put on his ornaments. For the LORD had said to Moses, "Say to the people of Israel, 'You are a stiff-necked people; if for a single moment I should go up among you, I would consume you. So now take off your ornaments, that I may know what to do with you.'" Therefore the people of Israel stripped themselves of their ornaments, from Mount Horeb onward.

Now Moses used to take the tent and pitch it outside the camp, far off from the camp, and he called it the tent of meeting. And everyone who sought the LORD would go out to the tent of meeting, which was outside the camp. Whenever Moses went out to the tent, all the people would rise up, and each would stand at his tent door, and watch Moses until he had gone into the tent. When Moses entered the tent, the pillar of cloud would descend and stand at the entrance of the tent, and the LORD would speak with Moses. And when all the people saw the pillar of cloud standing at the entrance of the tent, all the people would rise up and worship, each at his tent door. Thus the LORD used to speak to Moses face to face, as a man speaks to his friend. When Moses turned again into the camp, his assistant Joshua the son of Nun, a young man, would not depart from the tent.

Moses said to the LORD, "See, you say to me, 'Bring up this people,' but you have not let me know whom you will send with me. Yet you have said, 'I know you by name, and you have also found favor in my sight.' Now therefore, if I have found favor in your sight, please show me now your ways, that I may know you in order to find favor in your sight. Consider too that this nation is your people." And he said, "My presence will go with you, and I will give you rest." And he said to him, "If your presence will not go with me, do not bring us up from here. For how shall it be known that I have found favor in your sight, I and your people? Is it not in your going with us, so that we are distinct, I and your people, from every other people on the face of the earth?"

And the LORD said to Moses, "This very thing that you have spoken I will do, for you have found favor in my sight, and I know you by name." Moses said, "Please show me your glory." And he said, "I will make all my goodness pass before you and will proclaim before you my name 'The LORD.' And I will be gracious to whom I will be gracious, and will show mercy on whom I will show mercy. But," he said, "you cannot see my face, for man shall not see me and live." And the LORD said, "Behold, there is a place by me where you shall stand on the rock, and while my glory passes by I will put you in a cleft of the rock, and I will cover you with my hand until I have passed by. Then I will take away my hand, and you shall see my back, but my face shall not be seen."

The LORD said to Moses, "Cut for yourself two tablets of stone like the first, and I will write on the tablets the words that were on the first tablets, which you broke. Be ready by the morning, and come up in the morning to Mount Sinai, and present yourself there to me on the top of the mountain. No one shall come up with you, and let no one be seen throughout all the mountain. Let no flocks or herds graze opposite that mountain." So Moses cut two tablets of stone like the first. And he rose early in the morning and went up on Mount Sinai, as the LORD had commanded him, and took in his hand two tablets of stone. The LORD descended in the cloud and stood with him there, and proclaimed the name of the LORD. The LORD passed before him and proclaimed, "The LORD, the LORD, a God merciful and gracious, slow to anger, and abounding in steadfast love and faithfulness, keeping steadfast love for thousands, forgiving iniquity and transgression and sin, but who will by no means clear the guilty, visiting the iniquity of the fathers on the children and the children's children, to the third and the fourth generation." And Moses quickly bowed his head toward the earth and worshiped. And he said, "If now I have found favor in your sight, O Lord, please let the Lord go in the midst of us, for it is a stiff-necked people, and pardon our iniquity and our sin, and take us for your inheritance."

And he said, "Behold, I am making a covenant. Before all your people I will do marvels, such as have not been created in all the earth or in any nation. And all the people among whom you are shall see the work of the Lord, for it is an awesome thing that I will do with you.

And the Lord said to Moses, "Write these words, for in accordance with these words I have made a covenant with you and with Israel." So he was there with the Lord forty days and forty nights. He neither ate bread nor drank water. And he wrote on the tablets the words of the covenant, the Ten Commandments.

When Moses came down from Mount Sinai, with the two tablets of the testimony in his hand as he came down from the mountain, Moses did not know that the skin of his face shone because he had been talking with God. Aaron and all the people of Israel saw Moses, and behold, the skin of his face shone, and they were afraid to come near him. But Moses called to them, and Aaron and all the leaders of the congregation returned to him, and Moses talked with them. Afterward all the people of Israel came near, and he commanded them all that the Lord had spoken with him in Mount Sinai. And when Moses had finished speaking with them, he put a veil over his face.

Whenever Moses went in before the Lord to speak with him, he would remove the veil, until he came out. And when he came out and told the people of Israel what he was commanded, the people of Israel would see the face of Moses, that the skin of Moses' face was shining. And Moses would put the veil over his face again, until he went in to speak with him.

DAY 1

The Overview

Exodus 32:30–35; 33:1–23;
34:1–10, 27–35

Thus the LORD used to speak to Moses face to face, as a man speaks to his friend. . . . And he said, "My presence will go with you, and I will give you rest." And he said to him, "If your presence will not go with me, do not bring us up from here. For how shall it be known that I have found favor in your sight, I and your people? Is it not in your going with us, so that we are distinct, I and your people, from every other people on the face of the earth?" And the LORD said to Moses, "This very thing that you have spoken I will do, for you have found favor in my sight, and I know you by name." (Ex. 33:11, 14–17)

The purpose of today's reading is to get focused on the basic facts of the story that we will be studying in detail. Did you get a sense of the intensity of Moses' prayers and the determined and almost reckless way he approached God? He was a man with whom the Lord spoke "face to face, as a man speaks to his friend" (33:11). He wanted to know God and find favor in his sight (33:13). But that was not enough. Moses would not stop praying until he secured the continued presence of God, not only for himself, but also for the people he was leading (33:15). And even that was not enough—Moses went on to make the extraordinary request, "Please show me your glory" (33:18).

As we approach this remarkable passage, focusing in on these few verses gives us more than enough to think about. However, no teaching in Scripture can be taken in isolation. Almost as though retracting a zoom lens, we need to move our perspective back to see how this meeting with God is set into a larger picture. For example, Israel's sin of dancing around the golden calf (Ex. 32) is basic to understanding the passage. The grace to be revealed shines all the brighter in contrast to the shocking evil in the hearts of the people. But the golden calf incident also needs to be put in context. We need to consider the whole book of Exodus to appreciate what is going on between God and Moses.

Exodus is nothing less than the story of salvation by grace alone. That doctrine is stated in the New Testament, but in Exodus it is presented in exciting narrative with dramatic pictures that have been with us from childhood. God Almighty heard the cries of the helpless children of Israel and did battle with the most powerful nation on earth to set them free. God carried them "on eagles' wings" and brought them to himself at the mountain of Sinai with the intention of making them into his "treasured possession" (19:4–5). There, from the mountain, he spoke to them and gave them ten basic "words" by which they could enjoy the liberty that he had purchased for them. He then not only obligated himself to them by way of a covenant, but he also promised his presence to a degree unknown by any nation of people on the face of the earth. All these thoughts need to be looked into to make Moses' meeting with God all the more meaningful.

The final aspect of context that must be appreciated, if our passage is to have its full meaning, is the perspective of the New

Testament. Even the exquisite glimpse of the glory of God given to Moses was only prologue to the coming of Jesus Christ and the privileges that are given to those who are in Christ. But it is important to begin our reflection with the basic facts of the passage as well as an awareness of the larger context. Then pray with anticipation that God will be pleased to teach you experimentally (as the Puritans would say) the realities behind the facts.

DAY 2

A Greater Glory

Exodus 34:29–35; 2 Corinthians 3:7–18

Aaron and all the people of Israel saw Moses, and behold,
the skin of his face shone, and they were afraid to come near
him. . . . And when Moses had finished speaking with them, he
put a veil over his face. Whenever Moses went in before the
LORD to speak with him, he would remove the veil, until he
came out. (Ex. 34:30, 33–34)

And we all, with unveiled face, beholding the glory of the Lord,
are being transformed into the same image from one degree of
glory to another. For this comes from the Lord who is the Spirit.
(2 Cor. 3:18)

Moses' face was shining as he came down the mountain with
the tablets of the testimony. He had to cover his face with a veil
because the people were in awe. Did you notice that the apostle
Paul gives a very different perspective on Moses' use of the veil
from that which comes from a reading of Exodus alone? In Exodus
we are struck by the radiance on the face of Moses that came from
being in the presence of God. It caused the people to be in awe of

Moses and became a powerful reminder of his unique standing before God. Paul, on the other hand, interprets that same incident to demonstrate the superiority of the new covenant ("ministry of the Spirit") over the old. The glory of the old was a fading glory in comparison to the surpassing and permanent glory of the new.

We will consider both passages in detail in later meditations, but it is important to get a taste of the teaching of the New Testament as we begin. We live today in the blessing of the new covenant, or the New Testament, as we call the record of that covenant. All of the shadows and promises that are found in the Old Testament point to the New, and specifically to their fulfillment in Jesus Christ. Therefore, as much as we benefit from the teaching of the Old Testament, it can only be fully understood and appreciated in the light of the New. The veil was taken away *historically* with the coming of Christ, and it is taken away *personally* when we turn to the Lord (2 Cor. 3:14–16). This new reality will be illustrated again and again as we proceed through these studies. It is striking to learn how often this incident and the role of Moses are mentioned in the New Testament. In each case, after due respect is given to Moses and the revelation he received, the New Testament writer goes on to show a greater fulfillment in the person of Christ.

The lesson is not only the matter of the primacy of the New Testament witness—it is also the fact that the anchor of our whole existence is found in Jesus Christ. This understanding will keep us from feeling that we are somehow meant to duplicate the experience of Moses in our own lives. There are wonderful lessons to be learned, but invariably they will cause us to focus more deeply on Jesus and the "glory that surpasses it" through our union with him.

Nevertheless, while we recognize that our union with Christ carries us to higher spiritual privilege than that of Moses or any other "saint" of the Old Testament, we must still question the actual reality of this in our own lives. Whether or not the radiance on Moses' face was relatively transient, the fact is that his time with God had changed him in a way that was apparent to others. Is our relationship with Christ apparent to others? Moses may have known God at a lesser level of revelation than we have in Christ. Yet he sustained that relationship day after day in such a way that he could be bold in his praying. Do we know that kind of boldness in our praying, since Christ Jesus as our high priest gives us even greater access? "We are very bold," says the apostle (2 Cor. 3:12). Are we? There is obviously a great deal to learn from Moses.

DAY 3

The First Meeting

Exodus 3:1–15

And the angel of the LORD appeared to him in a flame of fire out of the midst of a bush. He looked, and behold, the bush was burning, yet it was not consumed. And Moses said, "I will turn aside to see this great sight, why the bush is not burned." When the LORD saw that he turned aside to see, God called to him out of the bush, "Moses, Moses!" And he said, "Here I am." (Ex. 3:2–4)

Today's reading is the familiar account of Moses' meeting God at the burning bush. It was important as Moses' first meeting with God, but it is also foundational for the meetings that follow. This initial revelation began while Moses was in the desert happily tending the flocks of his father-in-law, minding his own business. I suspect that upon first leaving Egypt, Moses, like many of us who get away from the attractions of a cosmopolitan life, was restless and horrified at the prospect of spending the rest of his life in exile in the desert. But with the passage of time and the coming of his children, he most likely came to love the solitude and unhurried pace of his life and couldn't imagine how he could ever go back to the "rat race" of Egypt.

But God had other plans. The first thing to note in the passage is the fact that this initial meeting came about entirely at God's initiative. God used the burning bush as a device to arouse Moses' curiosity and then "called" (v. 4) Moses to himself. This initiative on the part of God is the pattern throughout Scripture, from his seeking out Adam and Eve after the fall, to the call that God graciously extends to draw us to faith in Christ ("by whom you were called into the fellowship of his Son, Jesus Christ our Lord" [1 Cor. 1:9; see also 1:20–31]). In subsequent meetings it will be Moses' seeking God, but it all goes back to God's coming to him.

A. W. Tozer's classic work, *The Pursuit of God*, begins on this same note:

> We pursue God because, and only because, He has first put an urge within us that spurs us to the pursuit. . . . And it is by this very prevenient drawing that God takes from us every vestige of credit for the act of coming. The impulse to pursue God originates with God, but the outworking of that impulse is our following hard after Him; and all the time we are pursuing Him, we are already in His hand.[1]

The relationship between the divine initiative and our response will always be mysterious. But a fundamental step to "the pursuit of God," as Tozer terms it, is to surrender the notion that we are the initiators, that something within us has the power to open heaven and take us into the presence of God.

It all begins with God. We already know that, deep in our hearts, if we have come to trust in Jesus. We know that God sought us, showed us our need, and gave us eyes of faith to behold

---

1. A. W. Tozer, *The Pursuit of God* (Camp Hill, PA: Christian Publications, 1982), 11–12.

our Savior. But in the actual practice of the Christian life, we constantly slide back toward the supposed self-sufficiency that took us away from God in the first place.

No matter the spiritual heights to which Moses climbed, he always knew it started when God came to him and called him to himself. We must never forget that same lesson. Reflect on this wonderful hymn of testimony:

I sought the Lord, and afterward I knew
He moved my soul to seek him, seeking me;
It was not I that found, O Savior true;
No, I was found of thee.

Thou didst reach forth thy hand and mine enfold;
I walked and sank not on the storm-vexed sea
—'Twas not so much that I on thee took hold,
As thou, dear Lord, on me.

I find, I walk, I love, but O the whole of love
Is but my answer, Lord to thee;
For thou wert long before-hand with my soul,
Always thou lovedst me.

—ANONYMOUS (1878)

DAY 4

"I Am Who I Am"

Exodus 3:13–15; 6:1–8

Then Moses said to God, "If I come to the people of Israel and say to them, 'The God of your fathers has sent me to you,' and they ask me, 'What is his name?' what shall I say to them?" God said to Moses, "I AM WHO I AM." And he said, "Say this to the people of Israel, 'I AM has sent me to you.' . . . This is my name forever, and thus I am to be remembered throughout all generations. . . . Say therefore to the people of Israel, 'I am the LORD, and I will bring you out from under the burdens of the Egyptians, and I will deliver you from slavery to them, and I will redeem you with an out-stretched arm and with great acts of judgment.'" (Ex. 3:13–15; 6:6)

The first part of today's reading is a continuation of Moses' meeting with God at the burning bush. He obeyed God, returned to Egypt, and spoke to the elders of Israel, and then he and Aaron had their first meeting with Pharaoh. Both meetings failed to elicit the response Moses hoped for. The workload for the people was increased and the elders complained bitterly. The second part of the reading takes place as a discouraged Moses returns to God for an explanation of what was going on (5:22–23).

God himself initiated the first meeting with Moses when he called him to the burning bush. Now we need to try to understand just *what* God revealed in that meeting. Essentially the purpose of the meeting was for God to reveal his name to Moses (3:13). That sounds strange at first because we are used to a name being simply a tag that we use to identify one person from another. But in Scripture, as well as in many cultures, a name is in reality a description of a person's features or character. The name is not just who they are, but what they are like. Taking the time to notice what name is used for God will profoundly impact your reading of the Bible.

In this instance God reveals his name as "the LORD." It is not as though he is a new God; he is the same as the God of Moses' ancestors (3:15). But as he explained in the later conversation recorded in chapter 6, there is something that those fathers did not know. "God" or even "God Almighty" (6:3) is a general name for God used by all peoples. On the other hand, when God entered into a covenant with the family of Abraham, the people he had chosen, he used a name that could only be rightfully used within the family. Throughout the Old Testament, this name is used as God deals with his covenant people. However, when Gentiles become involved, the name is no longer used, and the text reverts to the more general name, God. (See this in Daniel 2, for example.)

It is important to stop and reflect on this name. The place to start is to note that the Hebrew letters for God's covenant name are YHWH. Because of the sacredness of this name to the Jews, they would not corrupt even the letters by adding vowels to the text as it came later to be copied and recopied. For that reason, the actual pronunciation of the name has been lost. If two vowels are added, it is pronounced *YaHWeH*, which is commonly done today. The more traditional word, *YeHoWaH*, or *Jehovah*, is derived by adding three vowels. This gets even more complicated because in most of our English translations this name appears as "LORD" written in the uppercase. Note that this is a different name for God from "Lord" in lowercase letters (which carries the sense of "Lord and Master"). Understanding this will put a whole new light on reading the Old Testament and, in particular, will help make more sense of texts such as "O LORD, our Lord, how majestic is your name in all the earth" (Ps. 8:1), i.e., "O Yahweh, our Master . . ."

Now look again at 6:2–4, where God tells Moses that he is YHWH ("the LORD"), even though he didn't reveal himself in that way to Abraham, Isaac, and Jacob when he made his covenant with them. That statement has always puzzled me. In a passage such as Genesis 15 where the LORD made the covenant with Abraham, he does come as "the LORD" and is even called that by Abraham. What does it mean then, to say they didn't know him as the LORD? The answer lies in the words that follow in 6:6–8 where the LORD described what he would do to actually fulfill the promises of his covenant: he would fight for his people to redeem them from their slavery. So Abraham had *heard* the words of the covenant, but the *reality* of the covenant promises was about to be seen in the mighty acts of God. Perhaps we could say that Abraham knew God as LORD *theologically* but that Moses and the people of Israel were about to come to know him as LORD *experientially*. It was now time for the revelation of this name in a greater fullness.

In Exodus 33:19 the Lord proclaimed his name, the LORD, to Moses in an even fuller sense. But between the revelation of chapter 6 and that of chapter 33 there had to be time and experiences to allow the earlier revelation to become a reality. Still later there would be an even more profound revelation of that "name that is above every name" (Phil. 2:9), the name of Jesus, but that, too, needed to await the proper time.

As we seek to know the Lord in a deeper sense, we have to ask ourselves if this is simply a theological or intellectual quest. Do we know experientially even the more elementary understanding of God that we already have? If not, what value would there be in a greater revelation? Somehow our theoretical and factual knowledge of God has to match up with our experience of him, or we get out of balance. It seems to me that the Lord knows that better than we, which is why he brings us step-by-step to the place where we are ready to take in the deeper lessons.

DAY 5

Redemption by Grace

Exodus 6:6–8; 12:1–13

Say therefore to the people of Israel, "I am the LORD, and I will bring you out from under the burdens of the Egyptians, and I will deliver you from slavery to them, and I will redeem you with an outstretched arm and with great acts of judgment. I will take you to be my people, and I will be your God, and you shall know that I am the LORD your God, who has brought you out from under the burdens of the Egyptians. I will bring you into the land that I swore to give to Abraham, to Isaac, and to Jacob. I will give it to you for a possession. I am the LORD." (Ex. 6:6–8)

The great promises of redemption in chapter 6 are demonstrated in the terrible judgment spoken of in the reading in chapter 12 as well as in the actual death of the firstborn (12:29–32) and the crossing of the Red Sea (13:17–14:31). I have a very distinct memory of studying the story of the exodus as a graduate student. Like a light bulb going on, I realized that virtually every detail of God's deliverance of his people was a picture of "by grace you have been saved" (Eph. 2:5, 8). It was one of those moments of enlightenment that permanently affected my understanding of

God. From that time on I have seen the Bible as a unity and the God who met with Moses as the same One whom I meet through Jesus Christ. I'm sure I already understood this *theologically* (to use the terminology of the last lesson), but now this great truth became mine *experientially*.

I mention this insight because I continue to meet many Christians who have not taken this step in understanding the Old Testament. They see the Old Testament as full of wonderful stories (and puzzles) but see its teaching as that which relates to a totally different era. There are important differences to be sure, but those differences relate to a very different context, not to the character of God or the way he saves us. Grace is as fundamental to the Old Testament as it is to the New.

Now go back and read Exodus 6:6 with your own spiritual condition in mind. Aren't we also slaves and in such an oppressed condition that we are helpless to change our situation? In Ephesians 2:1–3, we are said to be dead in our trespasses and sins. The hope is not that we somehow resolve to be different, but that "God, being rich in mercy, because of the great love with which he loved us, even when we were dead in our trespasses, *made us alive* together with Christ" (Eph. 2:4–5). Do you see the very same mercy at work in the saving of Israel from its bondage—"I will deliver you from slavery to them, and I will redeem you with an outstretched arm and with great acts of judgment" (Ex. 6:6)?

The key word in that statement is the word *redeem*. Redemption is virtually synonymous with salvation. However, it adds the idea of a purchase price or ransom. God did not simply take his people away; he redeemed them, and the price he paid was the blood of the innocent lamb. In the reading from Exodus 12, recall that the Lord said Israel was to begin its calendar from the date of the slaying of the lamb. Their life of freedom began with their redemption through the death of the Passover lamb (12:2). Jesus is that Passover Lamb, and just as Israel returned every year to celebrate their new beginning in freedom from slavery, so we come again and again to the communion table. There we acknowledge that we are free from the curse of sin because of the cross of Jesus.

Return to the reading in Exodus 6 and read verse 7 again. "I will take you to be my people, and I will be your God" is the essence of the covenant of grace. The Lord spoke those words to Abraham (Gen. 17:7–8), then again here in Exodus, and again as part of the new covenant (Jer. 31:33; Heb. 8:10). God Almighty himself comes to sinful people and obligates himself to be with them and to save them. And there is nothing those people did or could do to deserve that level of commitment. That was true for Israel and it is true for us. The only way salvation has ever come has been through the grace of God.

A final thought from this lesson comes from verse 7 where God says, "and you shall know that I am the LORD your God." We will come back again and again to this word *know*. To know God as the LORD, the God who comes personally to save us and be with us, has many dimensions. But it begins with our acknowledging joyfully and gratefully that we have been saved by grace alone, and however unworthy we may feel, God has been pleased to save us through his Son, Jesus. We contributed nothing to that gracious act, nor can we add anything to it now. If you haven't fully appreciated that in your own experience, you can see it fully displayed in the salvation of Israel. Our God is gracious!

> Amazing grace, how sweet the sound
> That saved a wretch like me;
> I once was lost, but now am found,
> Was blind, but now I see.

—JOHN NEWTON (1779)

The Ten Words

Exodus 19:16–20; 20:1–21

On the morning of the third day there were thunders and lightnings and a thick cloud on the mountain and a very loud trumpet blast, so that all the people in the camp trembled. Then Moses brought the people out of the camp to meet God, and they took their stand at the foot of the mountain. Now Mount Sinai was wrapped in smoke because the LORD had descended on it in fire. The smoke of it went up like the smoke of a kiln, and the whole mountain trembled greatly. . . . The LORD came down on Mount Sinai, to the top of the mountain. And the LORD called Moses to the top of the mountain, and Moses went up. (Ex. 19:16–18, 20)

And God spoke all these words, saying, "I am the LORD your God, who brought you out of the land of Egypt, out of the house of slavery." . . . Moses said to the people, "Do not fear, for God has come to test you, that the fear of him may be before you, that you may not sin." (Ex. 20:1–2, 20)

No set of statements or commandments has been so revered and studied (or vilified) as the words we know as the Ten

Commandments. And this is appropriate. These commandments, unlike any other law given to Israel, were spoken by a voice that could be heard by the people themselves. (If this does not seem to be clear in Exodus 20, it is explicitly stated in Deuteronomy 4:11–13 and 5:4, 22, where Moses recounts this event for a new generation.) It is little wonder that they were terrified and begged Moses to be the messenger through whom they would hear the Law (20:18–19). It was these same "Ten" that were recopied when Moses returned to the mountain in chapter 34. They were then placed in the ark of the covenant as a perpetual witness to the people of the character of their God.

The Old Testament abounds in laws, commands, and decrees, but these ten clearly stand out as the Law from which all the other laws are derived. In fact, the Ten are not even called "commandments" in Scripture. They are literally the "ten words," even though the usual English translation is "commandments" (see Ex. 32:16; 34:28; Deut. 4:13; 10:4, where they are also called the "covenant" or the "testimony"). There is no end of thoughts that could be offered about the Ten. But for the purpose of a deeper appreciation of what transpired in Moses' second trip up the mountain, reconsider the setting in which the Ten were given. Reflect on the fact that redemption by grace alone had occurred well before they were spoken. God's saving his people from bondage had nothing whatsoever to do with the Law. It was accomplished by his mighty power and through the sacrifice of the Passover Lamb.

In his first meeting with Moses at the base of Sinai, the Lord told him that once the people had been delivered, Moses would lead them back to the very place where they were meeting (Ex. 3:12). Now they were there, still infants in their faith, not even sure if being saved from the bondage of Egypt was better than the life they knew before. They were God's people because of a mighty act of grace done in their lives. But they didn't *know* what that meant, and they didn't know the God who had saved them. And so God graciously came to meet with them. As Moses later interpreted this event, he explained, "Has any god ever attempted to go and take a nation for himself from the midst of another nation . . . by a mighty hand and an outstretched arm. . . . To you it was shown, that you might know that the LORD is God; there is no other besides him" (Deut. 4:34–35). He made it clear that the Lord's intention in giving the "ten words" was not to be punitive, but to give them a basic direction "that it may go well with you and with your children after you" (Deut. 4:40). All of Deuteronomy 4 and 5 is a marvelous commentary on the meaning of Exodus 20 and the giving of the Law.

Once again we are encountering the God of grace and mercy. Even in the actual giving of the Ten, he began with a reminder of his unconditional love: "I am the LORD your God, who brought you out of the land of Egypt, out of the house of slavery" (Ex. 20:2). In the words that follow, he gave ten unambiguous statements that he expected to be obeyed. He spoke as a loving father would to children who need simple but firm directions for their own good (see Deut. 10:10–13). The Lord had a life of unspeakable joy and fulfillment for his people. It was his plan to make them his "treasured possession" (Ex. 19:5). But this could never be experienced until they learned to obey. Knowing God includes obedience. Here at Sinai the people of God were introduced to that essential lesson.

Do we ever get away from the need to come back to these first lessons? We are not saved by obedience; we are saved by grace. But we will only know what that means and know the God who saved us by coming to him in a spirit of obedience. There is a significant difference in the degree of freedom we have under the new covenant. Under the Law covenant, God's people were treated as little children—because that is what they were. We have "come of age" and have entered into our full rights as heirs (Gal. 4:4–7). But the fact that we have been given "freedom" in Christ (Gal. 5:1) doesn't take away from the need to come to God with a childlike spirit of submission and genuine desire for obedience. "Do not use your freedom as an opportunity for the flesh, but through love serve one another. For the whole law is fulfilled in one word: 'You shall love your neighbor as yourself'" (Gal. 5:13–14).

Take some time in prayer to reaffirm your willingness to be obedient. The refrain of the familiar gospel song points the way to enjoying the salvation we have been given:

> Trust and obey, for there's no other way
> To be happy in Jesus, but to trust and obey.

—JOHN H. SAMMIS (1887)

DAY 7

The Presence of God

Exodus 24:1–25:9

Then he said to Moses, "Come up to the LORD . . . and worship from afar. Moses alone shall come near to the LORD, but the others shall not come near, and the people shall not come up with him." . . . Then Moses and Aaron, Nadab, and Abihu, and seventy of the elders of Israel went up, and they saw the God of Israel. There was under his feet as it were a pavement of sapphire stone, like the very heaven for clearness. . . . The LORD said to Moses, "Speak to the people of Israel, that they take for me a contribution. . . . And let them make me a sanctuary, that I may dwell in their midst." (Ex. 24:1–2, 9–10; 25:1–2, 8)

There is another concept that is vital to understand as we seek to appreciate Moses' meeting with God in Exodus 32–34. That is the idea of the "Presence" of God that is introduced in the reading for today. It is this Presence that is the object of Moses' tenacious intercession in those chapters. In 33:15 he prayed: "If your Presence will not go with me, do not bring us up from here" (I will capitalize the word to make it distinct from the truth that God is everywhere present).

After God gives specific case law as applications of the Ten (chaps. 21–23), there is a ceremony in God's presence that seals the covenant relationship with blood and a meal (24:1–11). Our reading says that the elders "saw the God of Israel" (24:10) and "beheld God, and ate and drank" (24:11). Later the Lord would say to Moses, "Man shall not see me and live" (33:20), so this has to be a different kind of seeing, perhaps limited to God's "feet." Nevertheless the elders enjoyed an extraordinary meal in the very Presence of God.

Moses was then called up into Mount Sinai for forty days and nights (24:18). During that time he was given detailed instruction about the construction of the tabernacle (chaps. 25–31). This included not only the furniture, but the minutest detail about the tent itself, the area around the tent, the garments of the priests who would offer sacrifices, and even the formula for the incense to be used in tabernacle ceremonies. A first reading through all of this detail seems to call attention preeminently to the holiness of God—the Most Holy Place that could be entered only by a high priest who himself had been cleansed; the necessity of blood sacrifice done in the prescribed manner; the constant threats for any aberration, etc. The other aspect about the tabernacle that draws so much comment is that every aspect of it points in one way or another to the person and work of our ultimate high priest, Jesus Christ. But while both of these lessons are basic to the meaning of the tabernacle, there is an even more fundamental truth that must first be considered.

In his introductory words to the description of the tabernacle, the Lord says this: "And let them make me a sanctuary, *that I may dwell in their midst*" (25:8). Later he says: "There I will meet with the people of Israel, and it shall be sanctified by my glory . . . I will dwell among the people of Israel and will be their God. And they shall know that I am the LORD their God, who brought them out of the land of Egypt that I might dwell among them. I am the LORD their God" (29:43, 45–46).

While all of the specifics of the tabernacle were to teach visibly aspects of the character of God, the fundamental reality was that he had chosen to come and literally dwell in their midst. Moses or his successors would no longer need to leave the camp and climb the mountain to talk to God—he would be in its center, living where they lived, living how they lived—in a tent. "There I will meet with you, and from above the mercy seat, from between the two cherubim that are on the ark of the testimony, I will speak with you about all that I will give you in commandment for the people of Israel" (25:22). Throughout the revelation of the building of the tabernacle, the most common term used was the *tent of meeting* (27:21; 28:43; 29:10, 42, 44, etc.). Once the camp was established and the tabernacle erected, that Presence in the center of the camp was demonstrated by the sight of a cloud by day and a pillar of fire at night (40:34–38).

What an extraordinary thing—to have the Lord of heaven and earth living among his people! As Moses later prayed, this is what distinguished the Israelites from all other people on the face of the earth (33:16). Of course they knew that he was omnipresent and that they couldn't contain him (this is the deception of idolatry—that a god is now in the possession of his owners), but they also were to understand that he had chosen to come and be with them in this unique way. It is little wonder that God's threat to withdraw his Presence and give them a general blessing instead (33:1–6) was unacceptable to Moses and the people.

This theme of the presence of God unfolds through the rest of Scripture. When the people of God arrived in the Promised Land and lived in permanent dwellings instead of tents, the Lord decreed that he, too, would live in a house. He directed David and Solomon to build the great temple in Jerusalem. It is clear from Solomon's prayer of dedication that he understood this idea of Presence (2 Chron. 6:12–42).

When we come to the New Testament, the truth of God's Presence in the midst of his people is fulfilled first of all in the person of Jesus. A literal rendering of John 1:14 is "the Word became flesh and *tabernacled* ["lived for a while" NIV] among us." But if Jesus' earthly life was the more temporary earthly dwelling of God, represented by the tabernacle, then the permanent dwelling, the temple, is found in the gathering of the church (1 Cor. 3:16–17; Eph. 2:21–22). One way to understand the term *body of Christ*, as used for the church, is this concept of visible Presence.

God *still* dwells with his people. There will be unique times when we as individuals know that Presence. But the way to know that Presence in an ongoing sense is to gather with the people of God in worship, celebration, and prayer. God is there. If he is not, then there is nothing that makes us different from any other gathering of people. Let us continually seek his Presence together.

So then you are no longer strangers and aliens, but you are fellow citizens with the saints and members of the household of God, built on the foundation of the apostles and prophets, Christ Jesus himself being the cornerstone, in whom the whole structure, being joined together, grows into a holy temple in the Lord. In him you also are being built together into a dwelling place for God by the Spirit. (Eph. 2:19–22)

DAY 8

Sin Is Ugly

Exodus 32:1–20

When the people saw that Moses delayed to come down from the mountain, the people gathered themselves together to Aaron and said to him, "Up, make us gods who shall go before us. As for this Moses, the man who brought us up out of the land of Egypt, we do not know what has become of him." . . . And he received the gold from their hand and fashioned it with a graving tool and made a golden calf. . . . And the Lord said to Moses, "Go down, for your people, whom you brought up out of the land of Egypt, have corrupted themselves. They have turned aside quickly out of the way that I commanded them. They have made for themselves a golden calf and have worshiped it and sacrificed to it and said, 'These are your gods, O Israel, who brought you up out of the land of Egypt!'" (Ex. 32:1, 4, 7–8)

How could they do it? Reading the infamous story of the golden calf immediately makes us very critical of the children of Israel. How could they be so stupid and shortsighted? It is true that Moses had been gone over a month, and that is a long time when you have nothing to do but wait. But wouldn't the memory of the voice of God and the extraordinary experience they had shared at the base of this mountain sustain them for even that amount of time? Furthermore, it is not as though this was the first time they had a chance to reflect on the power of God at work on their behalf. They had all witnessed the plagues, including the ones they had been protected from (Exodus 7–10). They had participated in the Passover when their own firstborn sons were spared judgment (chaps. 11–12). They had watched the Red Sea part for them and close over their enemies (chap. 14). They had seen God graciously provide manna and quail and water (chaps. 16–17). And yet, in a fairly minor crisis, their faith completely failed, and they turned against the God that saved them.

We ask, "How could *they* do it?" as we reflect on the ugliness of their rebellion, as a way of asking, "How can *we* do it?" We have experienced the abundance of God's love through Christ, but we are constantly disobeying our Lord. And, in my experience, it seems that I am especially prone to falling just after I have been given a special blessing! In terms of serious progress in the spiritual life, I seem to have a death wish. Whenever I think I'm getting close to some sort of breakthrough, I do something to ruin my chances of getting closer to God. So I find the rebellion of Israel disgusting and inexcusable—not as a statement of judgment, but as a look into a mirror. I don't like what I see. What does this say to you?

Strange as it may seem, this terrible incident is integral to the remainder of the passage. There are important lessons here. First of all, we are reminded in looking at this *mirror* that all sin is, at its core, rebellion against God. Too often we focus on the sensual aspects of this event. But the "party" was the consequence of the people's perception that they now had God in their control. An alternative translation in 32:1, 4, and 8 for "gods" is "God," since the word for God is a plural word in the Hebrew (*Elohim*). In other words, Aaron probably wasn't offering them new gods, he was giving them their God in a form they could manage. Notice in verse 5 that he calls the festival to the golden calves a "feast to the LORD." And it was after doing their religious duty that they "rose up to play" (v. 6). Can it be that the grosser aspects of our flesh are always present just beneath the surface, and any movement away from the Lord allows them to appear? That seems evident in the character of societies, from the Israelites to our own culture. And this is also true for us. We need to face the reality of how ready we are to move in this direction.

We are also reminded in this passage that God, who sees the ugliness of sin far more clearly than we, nevertheless still came to dwell with his people. Sin must be dealt with, not only in terms of the immediate situation, as it was here, but in an ongoing sense, as provided through the sacrifices. But confession and forgiveness of sin did not change the root character of the people. *And yet he came!* In a very real sense, the richness of God's mercy could be seen to an even greater depth because of this uncovering of the depth of sin in the hearts of his people. This is not to suggest in any way that the sin of the people was good. But I do think that it was necessary to provide a contrasting background for the revelation that would follow.

It seems that reminders of the depth of our own sinfulness are necessary to appreciate more fully the depth and breadth of God's love for us. Paul's statement, "There is therefore now no condemnation for those who are in Christ Jesus" (Rom. 8:1), shines all the brighter in the light of the wrestling he had just done with his own depravity (Rom. 7:14–25). We need to heartily repent of our sin, but at the same time we need to give up the notion that in doing so we have made ourselves acceptable to a holy God. We are welcome in the presence of God because we are his children through our Lord and Savior Jesus Christ (see Rom.

8:1–17). One of the most fundamental battles of the spiritual life is to face the horror of sin but then, with no illusions about our own goodness, to marvel all the more at the richness of God's mercy that is ours through Jesus.

Nothing in my hand I bring, simply to the cross I cling;
Naked come to thee for dress; helpless look to thee for grace;
Foul, I to the Fountain fly; wash me Savior, or I die.

—Augustus M. Toplady (1776)

DAY 9

Intercessory Prayer

Exodus 32:21–35; Hebrews 4:14–16

The next day Moses said to the people, "You have sinned a great sin. And now I will go up to the LORD; perhaps I can make atonement for your sin." So Moses returned to the LORD and said, "Alas, this people has sinned a great sin. They have made for themselves gods of gold. But now, if you will forgive their sin . . ." (Ex. 32:30–32)

Since then we have a great high priest who has passed through the heavens, Jesus, the Son of God, let us holdfast our confession. . . . Let us then with confidence draw near to the throne of grace, that we may receive mercy and find grace to help in time of need. (Heb. 4:14, 16)

The readings today teach us the meaning of *intercessory* prayer— praying for others. One of the most challenging aspects of this study of Exodus is the intensity of Moses' intercession for Israel. But once again, the lessons learned from Moses point us to Jesus.

In Exodus 18, there is a record of the advice given by Moses' father-in-law, Jethro, as he watched Moses exhaust himself in trying to meet all the needs of the people. Moses needed to dele-gate most of the work to other capable men. But one duty he could not delegate, and the one mentioned first by Jethro, was that Moses would "represent the people before God" (18:19). That statement, along with the rest of the advice given (18:19–23), is a profound and compelling list of priorities for effective spiritual leadership. Moses' first forty days on the mountain certainly served as an example of his representing the people. But now, in the aftermath of the terrible sin of the Israelites, there comes into play another meaning of that call. In a literal, and almost physical, sense, Moses stands between God and the people. Moses so identified with the people, even in their sin, that if God was going to destroy them, then he was to be destroyed too—"please blot me out of your book that you have written" (32:32; see also Rom. 9:1–4 where Paul stated he was willing to accept damnation if it would mean the salvation of his people, the Jews).

It is this tenacious intercession that is the key to understanding the encounters that follow. In no case did Moses seek anything for his personal benefit. He was truly selfless in what he sought from God. And it will also become evident that God is both honored and pleased with this kind of bold prayer. We are often timid in the way we pray because, in the back of our minds, we wonder if we are not being selfish in asking for this or that blessing. And that may very well be the case! But when it comes to praying for others, we should pray with great boldness, because in the mysterious realm of prayer God Almighty is moved to act when his people pray.

The intercession of Moses is only one of dozens of examples in Scripture. This thought is also clearly confirmed in the teaching of Jesus about prayer. Consider, for example, his parable of the man who sought bread for his guests in Luke 11: "because of his *impudence* ["persistence" NIV] he will rise and give him whatever he needs" (Luke 11:8).

But in this important matter of intercessory prayer, it is crucial that we look finally, not at Moses' example or even the teaching of Jesus, but at the person of Jesus and what he does for us. The book of Hebrews, from which the second reading is taken, was written to move our minds from the lessons of the Old Testament to their fulfillment in Christ. "Therefore, holy brothers, you who share in a heavenly calling, consider Jesus, the apostle and high priest of our confession" (Heb. 3:1). And, as we read in chapter 4, there is no intercession like that of Jesus'. He not only offers a kind of intercession that Moses, though willing, was unable to do ("*perhaps* I can make atonement for your sin" [Ex. 32:30]), but his intercession continues to this very moment. The writer of Hebrews deliberately uses the present tense in saying we "have" a great high priest in the presence of God. Ultimately then, the mercy God bestows on the people we are praying for does not depend on our intercession but on the intercession of Jesus.

Nevertheless, it is important to notice that the application of this passage is that since Jesus is our high priest, we should "with confidence draw near to the throne of grace" so that we may receive the answers to our prayers (Heb. 4:16). Therefore, knowing that Jesus is our high priest does not remove the need to pray as Moses did. It opens the way to praying with even greater confidence than he had.

DAY 10

Full Atonement

Hebrews 2:14–3:6; 9:11–14; 10:19–23; Exodus 32:30

Therefore, holy brothers, you who share in a heavenly calling, consider Jesus, the apostle and high priest of our confession, who was faithful to him who appointed him, just as Moses also was faithful in all God's house. For Jesus has been counted worthy of more glory than Moses. . . . Now Moses was faithful in all God's house as a servant, to testify to the things that were to be spoken later, but Christ is faithful over God's house as a son. And we are his house if indeed we hold fast our confidence and our boasting in our hope. (Heb. 3:1–3, 5–6)

The next day Moses said to the people, "You have sinned a great sin. And now I will go up to the LORD; perhaps I can make atonement for your sin." (Ex. 32:30)

Reflect today on the intercession of Moses but in particular on the statement recorded in verse 30, "Perhaps I can make atonement for your sin." As dedicated an intercessor as Moses may have been, that was something *he could not do*. The Lord replied that he would render judgment when it was time (v. 34).

The idea behind atonement is that of removing an offense so there can be reconciliation with the one offended. Sin is offensive to God and puts a barrier between the sinner and God. The sense that such a barrier exists and that something needs to be done to remove it is a reality that haunts every human being—whether ancient or modern. But Moses' desire to do something to make atonement for the sins committed at Mount Sinai and the universal search for atonement both reveal the helplessness of mankind to bring down the barrier.

In fact, they point the way to the work of Jesus Christ on the cross. That is why reading from Exodus 32 took us to readings in the letter to the Hebrews. The writer emphasized over and over, often in contrast to the ministry of Moses, that the death of Jesus provided full atonement for our sin. He did what no animal sacrifice or human priest could ever do: "that he might make atonement for the sins of the people" (Heb. 2:17 NIV), "he has appeared once for all at the end of the ages to put away sin by the sacrifice of himself (9:26); "we have been made holy through the sacrifice of the body of Jesus Christ once for all" (10:10 NIV).

Without having a true appreciation of the atonement of Christ, it is not possible to boldly seek the face of God. It is certainly possible to be an ardent seeker after God without such an understanding, but when that is the case, the seeking will include either an inappropriate presumption (the "man upstairs" kind of thinking) or an underlying fear that we are unacceptable. On one level, the teaching on atonement is so basic that anyone who has come to faith in Christ has some understanding that Jesus died for our sins. But in too many instances we tend to view the atonement as the thing that got us in the front door. Afterward, however, we are on our own, and we need to do something more to gain worthiness and favor with God. But this contradicts the burden of Hebrews:

> Therefore, brothers, since we have confidence to enter the holy places by the blood of Jesus, by the new and living way that he opened for us through the curtain, that is, through his flesh, and since we have a great priest over the house of God, let us draw near with a true heart in full assurance of faith. (10:19–22)

Moses *wanted* to make atonement for the sins of the people—Jesus actually did it. This glorious truth is celebrated in the Scripture; we return to it every time we come to the communion table, and it needs to be alive for us every time we pray.

> Arise, my soul arise, shake off your guilty fears;
> The bleeding sacrifice in my behalf appears:
> Before the throne my Surety stands,
> My name is written on his hands.
>
> He ever lives above, for me to intercede,
> His all redeeming love, his precious blood to plead;
> His blood atoned for every race,
> And sprinkles now the throne of grace.
>
> My God is reconciled; his pardoning voice I hear,
> He owns me for his child, I can no longer fear;
> With confidence I now draw nigh,
> And "Father, Abba, Father!" cry.

—CHARLES WESLEY (1742)

The Absence of God

Exodus 33:1–6

The LORD said to Moses, "Depart; go up from here, you and the people whom you have brought up out of the land of Egypt, to the land of which I swore to Abraham, Isaac, and Jacob, saying, 'To your offspring I will give it.' I will send an angel before you, and I will drive out the Canaanites, the Amorites, the Hittites, the Perizzites, the Hivites, and the Jebusites. Go up to a land flowing with milk and honey; but I will not go up among you, lest I consume you on the way, for you are a stiff-necked people." When the people heard this disastrous word, they mourned, and no one put on his ornaments. (Ex. 33:1–4)

Can we be satisfied with the blessing of God if it comes without the presence of God? There is an important difference. Both Moses and the people understood that they were different and would not accept only the Lord's blessing. There is an important lesson here.

Notice that in 33:1, the Lord reaffirmed his promise to see that they would get back to their homeland. He promised protection from all their enemies through his angel and reminded them of the bounty that was there, the "land flowing with milk and honey" (vv. 2–3). All of this had been repeatedly stated, and here it is stated again. But then the Lord said something that was a radical change in his dealing with his people. Because of their rebellious nature, he said that he would not be going with them (v. 3). In fact it would not be good for them if he went—"If for a single moment I should go up among you, I would consume you" (v. 5). With that horrifying prospect, the people genuinely humbled themselves in repentance (vv. 4, 6), and Moses began his determined intercession to resecure the Presence (vv. 12–17).

It is frightening to consider that there can be blessing from God, even the material blessings of being in the land of milk and honey, without God's being there. We tend to think that obtaining those blessings indicates the presence of God. Furthermore, when we have those material blessings (health, a reasonably comfortable life, family, friends, etc.), then we are perfectly satisfied. We do not ask the hard questions about whether we are coming to know more of the actual presence of God. In terms of my calling as a pastor, I need to recognize that the church I lead can seem to be growing, prospering, and effectively ministering—all of which are certainly blessings from God—without experiencing the actual presence of the God we serve.

It is not a comforting thought, but often the Lord has to strip away the blessing in order to cause us to hunger more deeply for his presence. That must be because, in our immaturity, we have a hard time separating one from the other. A deepening spiritual maturity, therefore, includes learning to distinguish between God's blessings and God's presence and then seeking to deepen our knowledge of God irrespective of outward circumstances. Neither our comfort nor our lack of comfort is, in itself, a sign of the presence of God.

But if the more tangible thing, the blessing, is not the same as the presence of God, how can we actually know this presence? Is it a feeling? An experience? Just what does it mean to be in the presence of God? This is what is now before us in the meat of the passage.

To begin with, it seems clear that we need to have the genuine sense of horror expressed by both Moses and the people at the thought of God's absence. His presence was vastly more important to them than his blessing. As immature and rebellious as they were, they got the message. And when they got the message, they responded. They humbled themselves before God and stripped off their ornaments as a demonstration of their heartfelt repentance.

When Martin Luther posted his famous Ninety-Five Theses on the door of the Wittenberg church, the movement now called the Reformation was launched. The first of Luther's theses was this: "Our Lord and Master Jesus Christ, in saying 'Repent ye . . .' meant the whole of life of the faithful to be an act of repentance."[1]

Psalm 130 was Luther's favorite; let it be your prayer of desire and of humility.

> Out of the depths I cry to you, O LORD!
>   O Lord, hear my voice!
> Let your ears be attentive
>   to the voice of my pleas for mercy!
>
> If you, O LORD, should mark iniquities,
>   O Lord, who could stand?
> But with you there is forgiveness,
>   that you may be feared.

1. Henry Bettenson, ed., *Documents of the Christian Church* (London: Oxford University Press, 1963), 260.

I wait for the Lord, my soul waits,
  and in his word I hope;
my soul waits for the Lord
    more than watchmen for the morning,
    more than watchmen for the morning.

O Israel, hope in the Lord!
    For with the Lord there is steadfast love,
    and with him is plentiful redemption.
And he will redeem Israel
    from all his iniquities.

DAY 12

The Tent of Meeting

Exodus 33:7–11

Now Moses used to take the tent and pitch it outside the camp, far off from the camp, and he called it the tent of meeting. And everyone who sought the LORD would go out to the tent of meeting, which was outside the camp. Whenever Moses went out to the tent, all the people would rise up, and each would stand at his tent door, and watch Moses until he had gone into the tent. When Moses entered the tent, the pillar of cloud would descend and stand at the entrance of the tent, and the LORD would speak with Moses. And when all the people saw the pillar of cloud standing at the entrance of the tent, all the people would rise up and worship, each at his tent door. Thus the LORD used to speak to Moses face to face, as a man speaks to his friend. (Ex. 33:7–11)

Look again at the first verse of today's reading: "Now Moses *used* to take the tent and pitch it outside the camp" (33:7). The verses of this reading are written in a way that suggests this is an insertion to explain how Moses was in a place where the Lord could come to him. The verb "used" suggests the idea of a pattern that was a consistent part of Moses' life. He regularly went a short distance from the camp and set up a tent that became known as the *tent of meeting*. Even though that same term was used of the tabernacle, that tent of meeting had not yet been erected. In this passage the tent was an ordinary one, but it was a place where Moses would meet with God, probably as a witness of what would come for all the people. The people could only watch as "the pillar of cloud would descend and stand at the entrance of the tent, and the LORD would speak with Moses" (v. 9). Moses would be in God's presence and talk to the Lord "face to face, as a man speaks to his friend" (v. 11).

This is what we could call *the devotional habits of Moses*. It takes us one step further in answering the question of just how, from the human side, we can know the presence of God in the profound sense revealed in Exodus 33 and 34. The steps we have already seen include (1) an expressed horror at the prospect of his absence and (2) a genuine repentance of the spirit of rebellion (33:4–6). To this list add (3) a regular time of meeting with God.

We should not expect those occasional moments of profound awareness of God's presence if we are not consistently coming before him in prayer, reflection, and reading of the Word. I found this helpful paragraph in a published journal entry of the late Roman Catholic mystic Henri Nouwen called "Useless Prayers":

> The remarkable thing, however, is that sitting in the presence of God for one hour each morning—day after day, week after week, month after month—in total confusion and with myriad distractions radically changes my life. God, who loves me so much that he sent his only son not to condemn me but to save me, does not leave me waiting in the dark too long. I might think that each hour is useless, but after thirty or sixty or ninety such useless hours, I gradually realize that I was not as

alone as I thought; a very small, gentle voice has been speaking to me far beyond my noisy place. So: Be confident and trust in the Lord.[1]

In addition to the pattern of meeting with God, there is another important lesson in this record of the tent. It points to the need to have a place where we meet with God. This is not a specific holy place, such as the tabernacle was to become, but a place that emotionally and even physically tells us it is time to "be still, and know that I am God" (Ps. 46:10). For me, this has been a particular room and even a chair within that room. As I sit in that chair, I find it far easier for my spirit to calm down than if I just go to a random place to try to be still. I have found it difficult to have anything more than a superficial devotional life when I am traveling. If I am in a new location for a few days, then I can mentally identify a place to be still and reestablish my sense of meeting.

Perhaps I am strange in that need, but I suspect not. As long as we are bodies as well as spirits, the idea of *place* will be important. Was this part of Jesus' teaching that when we pray we are to enter our "closet" (Matt. 6:6 KJV)? Of course, the principal issue in that passage is the need to be private in our praying, but couldn't he also be suggesting that we need our own place to pray? Do you have a "tent of meeting," and do you regularly go there to speak with the Lord?

1. Henri Nouwen, *The Road to Daybreak: A Spiritual Journey* (New York: Image Books, 1990), 30.

DAY 13

Face to Face

Exodus 33:11; John 15:5–15

Thus the LORD used to speak to Moses face to face, as a man speaks to his friend. When Moses turned again into the camp, his assistant Joshua the son of Nun, a young man, would not depart from the tent. (Ex. 33:11)

"I am the vine; you are the branches. Whoever abides in me and I in him, he it is that bears much fruit, for apart from me you can do nothing. If anyone does not abide in me he is thrown away like a branch and withers; and the branches are gathered, thrown into the fire, and burned. If you abide in me, and my words abide in you, ask whatever you wish, and it will be done for you. By this my Father is glorified, that you bear much fruit and so prove to be my disciples. As the Father has loved me, so have I loved you. Abide in my love. If you keep my commandments, you will abide in my love, just as I have kept my Father's commandments and abide in his love. These things I have spoken to you, that my joy may be in you, and that your joy may be full. This is my commandment, that you love one another as I have loved you. Greater love has no one than this, that someone lay down his life for his friends.

You are my friends if you do what I command you. No longer
do I call you servants, for the servant does not know what his
master is doing; but I have called you friends, for all that I have
heard from my Father I have made known to you." (John 15:5–15)

Today we will consider the implications of this single sentence:
"Thus the LORD used to speak to Moses face to face, as a man
speaks to his friend." Is something like this possible for us? Or
was this something only Moses experienced? The words of Jesus
to his disciples on the night before his crucifixion, when he called
them his "friends," make it clear that this is for us as well.

It should first of all be pointed out that in the case of Moses,
his face-to-face meeting with the Lord was not intended to be
understood in a literal, physical sense. When Moses asked for
that, he was told, "you cannot see my face, for man shall not see
me and live" (33:20). "Face to face" refers then to the intimacy
with which Moses and God communed. God was present though
not visible; nevertheless, we are to have a mental picture of two
old friends sitting together, looking each other in the eyes, and
talking about anything that would come to mind. This was the
ongoing relationship that Moses increasingly experienced with
God. When the time came for Moses to press his case urgently
(33:12–18), he did not come to a stranger, nor did he speak with
someone whom he went to only in times of trouble and need.

Not many people in Scripture are called "friends of God." Moses
was one and Abraham was another (Isa. 41:8; James 2:23). This
fact deepens the meaning of Jesus' statement to his disciples, "No
longer do I call you servants . . . but I have called you friends" (John
15:15). This means that the intimacy of relationship that Moses
knew with God, while in some respects quite unique (Num. 12:8),
is nevertheless our privilege as well, through Jesus. We, too, can
know what it is to have a face-to-face relationship with the Lord.

In John 15 Jesus used another image that is not to be thought of as literal, but it is still quite remarkable in what it suggests. He called himself the vine and said that we are the branches. We are those who draw strength from Jesus so that by his energy we can bear fruit (15:5, 8). But the imagery of vine and branches also means we are intimately connected to him, are loved by him, can know his joy, and should think of him as our friend (15:9–15).

In *The Pursuit of God*, A. W. Tozer defines faith as "the gaze of a soul upon a saving God." Bring this definition to the picture of two friends sitting face-to-face and talking. It is by faith—the gaze of the soul upon a saving God—that we know he is present in the conversation. Let Tozer speak to us further on this matter:

> When we lift our inward eyes to gaze upon God we are sure to meet friendly eyes gazing back at us, for it is written that the eyes of the Lord run to and fro throughout all the earth. The sweet language of experience is "Thou God seest me." When the eyes of the soul looking out meet the eyes of God looking in, heaven has begun right here on this earth. When the habit of inwardly gazing Godward becomes fixed within us we shall be ushered onto a new level of spiritual life more in keeping with the promises of God and the mood of the New Testament. The Triune God will be our dwelling place even while our feet walk the low road of simple duty here among men. We will have found life's *summum bonum* indeed.

Note that Tozer speaks of "the habit of inwardly gazing Godward." That could be thought of in terms of our *duty* or *obligation* to have regular times of communion with God. We run away from those words in our day, but there are times when we don't feel like doing something and we do it anyway—because it is our *duty*. In this instance, however, this is an obligation to meet with a friend, and it is therefore a duty we anticipate with joy, just like we anticipate an evening with a friend whom we haven't seen for some time. How do we turn our duty into a delight? A key is to embrace Tozer's remark that as we enter God's presence and by faith seek to gaze upon him, we can be sure that we will "meet friendly eyes gazing back at us." Conclude this meditation by praying the prayer Tozer wrote at the end of the chapter entitled, "The Gaze of the Soul," from which the quotations were taken:

> O Lord, I have heard a good word inviting me to look away to Thee and be satisfied. My heart longs to respond, but sin has clouded my vision till I see Thee but dimly. Be pleased to cleanse me in Thine own precious blood, and make me inwardly pure, so that I may with unveiled eyes gaze upon Thee all the days of my earthly pilgrimage. Then shall I be prepared to behold Thee in full splendor in the day when Thou shalt appear to be glorified in Thy saints and admired in all them that believe. Amen.[1]

1. A. W. Tozer, *The Pursuit of God* (Camp Hill, PA: Christian Publications, 1982), 90–97.

DAY 14

Let Me Know You

Exodus 33:12–13

Moses said to the LORD, "See, you say to me, 'Bring up this people,' but you have not let me know whom you will send with me. Yet you have said, 'I know you by name, and you have also found favor in my sight.' Now therefore, if I have found favor in your sight, please show me now your ways, that I may know you in order to find favor in your sight. Consider too that this nation is your people." (Ex. 33:12–13)

Because of our previous studies, we know that the remarkable prayers recorded in 33:12–34:3 took place in the tent of meeting just outside the camp. The Lord still was not dwelling in the midst of his people as he promised, but he was coming nearer thanks to the powerful intercession of Moses. The people were aware of this, and they watched and worshiped as Moses met with the Lord in the tent (33:10). The prayer we read for today is Moses' response to the Lord's call for repentance in Exodus 33:5.

That the Lord threatened his absence and then came closer, and appeared to want to be asked to come even closer, should not be viewed as some kind of capriciousness on God's part. He had already declared by blood oath what he would do. But as part of his remarkable condescension, the Lord dealt with his people in a way in which they could participate as human beings. By studying Moses we can learn that God invites us to argue with him, to present our case, and to try to change his mind. Through the back and forth of these intercessions Moses was learning to know God, and his prayers became bolder and bolder. This was not the same man who tried to talk God out of a call to service just months earlier.

Notice that in verse 12 Moses quoted God's word back to him—twice. In the first instance, Moses claimed that although the Lord was sending him forth to lead the people, he hadn't said whom he would send with him. In fact, the Lord *had* said whom he was sending—it would be his angel (32:34). In a respectful way, Moses was refusing to accept the Lord's will! If they could not know the very presence of God, they would not leave (33:15–16). "I will not let you go unless you bless me," said Jacob as he wrestled with the angel of the Lord (Gen. 32:26). That same kind of determination can be seen in Moses. He would resecure the presence of God, and he would not let go until he got it.

The second time Moses quoted God's word back to God, he referred to the assurance he had received of God's favor. The favor was to be found in that he was known by name to God. Based on the fact of God's knowledge of him, Moses went on to pray in Exodus 33:13 that he might "know [him] in order to find favor in [his] sight." He then concluded this part of the prayer by reminding God of his covenantal relationship with his people: "Consider too that this nation is your people." They, too, had been favored by God, not because of their inherent worthiness, but because God had chosen to favor them. Moses would not release God from his covenant. Even at the end of the full revelation that God would give him on the mountain, Moses, the most determined intercessor until Christ, returned to hold God to his promise (34:9).

The core idea throughout these studies has been the remarkable truth that God knows his people and wants them to know him. It is time to give this more concentrated attention. No form of prayer has had a greater effect on my spiritual life than the prayers throughout Scripture that we would come to know God. The striking thing is that it is always on the lips of those who *already* know God! Moses was a man with whom God spoke "face to face, as a man speaks to his friend," and yet Moses still prayed to know him (33:11).

As we shall see, the same kind of praying is found constantly on the part of the apostle Paul. On one level, knowing God is synonymous with entering into eternal life. Jesus said, "And this is eternal life, that they know you the only true God, and Jesus Christ whom you have sent" (John 17:3). But the same word is also used of an ever-deepening relationship with God. Paul said, "I count everything as loss because of the surpassing worth of knowing Christ Jesus my Lord" (Phil. 3:8).

> Thus says the LORD: "Let not the wise man boast in his wisdom, let not the mighty man boast in his might, let not the rich man boast in his riches, but let him who boasts boast in this, that he understands and knows me, that I am the LORD who practices steadfast love, justice, and righteousness in the earth. For in these things I delight, declares the LORD." (Jer. 9:23–24)

DAY 15

God Knows Us

Isaiah 43:1–13; Exodus 33:12–13, 17

But now thus says the LORD,
he who created you, O Jacob,
    he who formed you, O Israel:
"Fear not, for I have redeemed you;
    I have called you by name, you are mine.
When you pass through the waters, I will be with you;
    and through the rivers, they shall not overwhelm you;
when you walk through fire you shall not be burned,
    and the flame shall not consume you.

. . . .

Because you are precious in my eyes,
    and honored, and I love you,
I give men in return for you,
    peoples in exchange for your life.
Fear not, for I am with you." (Isa. 43: 1–2, 4–5)

"You have said, 'I know you by name, and you have also found favor in my sight.' Now therefore, if I have found favor in your sight, please show me now your ways, that I may know you." . . .

And the LORD said to Moses, "This very thing that you have
spoken I will do, for you have found favor in my sight, and I
know you by name." (Ex. 33:12–13, 17)

We are looking more closely at the prayers of Moses and
others in Scripture for a deeper knowledge of God. Through
the years of wrestling with the meaning of such prayers, I have
come to the conviction that what we are actually asking for is
to enter into a knowledge that the Lord already has of us. In
Exodus 33, Moses prayed to know the Lord, and the Lord said
he would grant that request because he already knew Moses. To
say that God knew Moses by name points clearly to knowing in
the sense of relationship, not simply in the sense of informa-
tion. As we read in Jeremiah 9, if we have any boast, it is not
in our wealth or wisdom or strength. It is that we know the
Lord. But an even greater boast, if such a word is appropriate
for this, is that the Lord knows us. Here is our place to stand,
our resting place.

In passage after passage in Isaiah, particularly in chapters
40–49, the Lord sets forth his divine majesty, his mighty creative
power, and his faithfulness to all he has promised. And the
context of those glorious statements is the fact that his people
can find deepest comfort because this mighty and gracious Lord
knows them so intimately that he calls them by name. This is
particularly evident in the reading for today.

Fear not, for I have redeemed you;
    I have called you by name, you are mine.
When you pass through the waters, I will be with you;
    and through the rivers . . .
[and] through fire.

. . . .

For I am the LORD your God.

. . . .

You are precious in my eyes,
 and honored, and I love you,

. . . .

everyone who is called by my name. (43:1-4, 7)

Consider one other example from Isaiah:

Can a woman forget her nursing child,
 that she should have no compassion on the son of her womb?
Even these may forget,
 yet I will not forget you.
Behold, I have engraved you on the palms of my hands.
(49:15–16)

These and many similar passages reveal God's love for those whom he saves and are not to be limited to Israel. The same themes can be found in the New Testament as well. In John 10 Jesus spoke of his sheep:

He calls his own sheep by name. . . . I know my own and my own know me. . . . My sheep hear my voice, and I know them, and they follow me. I give them eternal life, and they will never perish, and no one will snatch them out of my hand. (John 10:3, 14, 27–28)

"We love because he first loved us" (1 John 4:19). This is not love in some undefined sense, but God's love that is personal and specific.

This gives light to the mysterious word *foreknowledge* or *fore-know*, which appears several times in the New Testament (Rom. 8:29, 11:2; 1 Peter 1:2). It was not simply that God knew about us beforehand, before we believed. God knew us in the sense we have seen all through the Scriptures—he knew us individually and personally, and he could call us by name. He did this long before we could call his name. This is the idea of *chosen-ness* that marked Israel's identity and marks ours as well—"What then shall we say to these things [God's foreknowledge and predestination]? If God is for us, who can be against us?" (Rom. 8:31).

It is basic, then, to recognize that our prayer for deeper knowledge is really a prayer to know him in the way that he already knows us. While God's knowledge of us is perfect, our knowledge of him will always be growing. This is evident from Paul's conclusion to his great tribute to love: "Now we see in a mirror dimly, but then face to face. Now I know in part; then I shall know fully, even as I have been fully known." (1 Cor. 13:12)

DAY 16

Paul's Great Passion

Philippians 3:1–14

Indeed, I count everything as loss because of the surpassing worth of knowing Christ Jesus my Lord. For his sake I have suffered the loss of all things and count them as rubbish, in order that I may gain Christ and be found in him, not having a righteousness of my own that comes from the law, but that which comes through faith in Christ, the righteousness from God that depends on faith—that I may know him and the power of his resurrection, and may share his sufferings, becoming like him in his death, that by any means possible I may attain the resurrection from the dead. (Phil. 3:8–11)

I have always thought of Moses and Paul as the two "giants" of Scripture—one for the Old Testament era and one for the New. Neither Moses nor Paul was the actual bearer of salvation. It was Abraham and his seed, Christ, who brought redemption. But it was Moses and then Paul who were God's instruments to set forth, in teaching and writing, the meaning of God's mighty work.

It is not at all surprising, then, to learn that Moses' great passion to know God is also found in Paul. Both of them had personal experience of God's first knowing them by name in a very specific sense. When the Lord called to Moses from the burning bush, he called out "Moses, Moses" (Ex. 3:4) just as he called out "Saul, Saul" (Acts 9:4) when he brought Saul of Tarsus to himself. This is not to suggest that God's ability to say their names was in itself extraordinary. But consider what it must have been like for those men to actually hear their names spoken by God. God knew them! Now they became passionate to know God to the greatest degree possible.

That passion to know is very evident in the reading for today. Philippians was one of four epistles Paul wrote from prison. When he wrote, Paul was facing the prospect of losing his life. But that was immaterial to the apostle, because for him "to live [was] Christ, and to die [was] gain" (Phil. 1:21). He had the same disregard for any of his impressive earthly credentials—he considered them "loss for the sake of Christ" (3:7). Furthermore, everything was a loss "because of the surpassing worth of knowing Christ Jesus my Lord" (3:8). In fact, in comparison to the knowledge of Christ, everything else was considered rubbish by Paul. (In the KJV, that word *rubbish* is translated "dung.") He wanted to move as far away from his own righteousness as possible and instead be found cloaked in the righteousness of Christ, which comes through faith. Paul's hunger to know Christ included knowing the power of his resurrection and even a readiness to share in his sufferings.

In verse 12, Paul was careful to admit that he had not yet obtained this level of knowledge, but he was pressing ahead "to make it my own, because Christ Jesus has made me his own." He was striving to obtain what was already his in Christ. What Paul has in mind here is the idea of that perfect knowledge which God already had of him. He was now pressing on ("straining forward to what lies ahead" [3:13]) to enter that knowledge even though it would only be perfect when he met Christ ("then I shall know fully, even as I have been fully known," 1 Cor. 13:12). This was the "prize" (3:14) for which Paul was striving. Nothing, in life or in death, was more important to Paul than knowing God through his Son, Jesus Christ. It should not be at all surprising that he had this same passion for those whom he taught.

Paul, like Moses, was called to be a point man for the advancement of the kingdom of God. With his intelligence, skill, and drive, I can picture him easily fitting in with a top executive team in politics or industry. He could take a church or ministry and offer leadership to make it a tremendous success. But once he came to know Christ on the Damascus road, all of that potential was subservient to his passion to enter more deeply into that knowledge. Many of us, on a much more modest scale, are called to some form of leadership in the work of the kingdom. There is so much to be done, so many important tasks to be accomplished for our Master. But do we *know* the one whom we seek to serve? That is the fundamental question. Paul, both in his example and teaching, brings us back to this time and time again.

DAY 17

Paul's Prayers for Knowledge

Colossians 1:9–14

And so, from the day we heard, we have not ceased to pray for you, asking that you may be filled with the knowledge of his will in all spiritual wisdom and understanding, so as to walk in a manner worthy of the Lord, fully pleasing to him, bearing fruit in every good work and increasing in the knowledge of God. May you be strengthened with all power, according to his glorious might, for all endurance and patience with joy, giving thanks to the Father, who has qualified you to share in the inheritance of the saints in light. (Col. 1:9–12)

Given Paul's great passion to know God more deeply, it should not be surprising that this was what he desired for other believers as well. When we study the prayers he recorded, that is exactly what we find. Paul's prayer for the Colossians is the first example we will consider.

The understanding of how central these prayers are became the bedrock of my own spiritual life and opened a path of discovery that continues to this day. That understanding grew out of a struggle, which I know is shared by most followers of Jesus, to live a life that seemed even remotely close to the life I felt God wanted me to live. My growing frustration was that the harder I tried, the worse I seemed to get. I was praying for help, for power, for Holy Spirit baptism, for *anything* that could help me be what I knew Christ wanted me to be. But as I read the Scriptures, I found myself drawn to the praying that the apostle Paul did for those under his care. In particular, I have been profoundly affected by the prayers in what are known as the four Prison Epistles: Ephesians, Philippians, Colossians, and Philemon. In every one of them, Paul introduced the letter by stating that he had been praying for those to whom he wrote. But beyond that general statement, he went on to say precisely what it was he had prayed for them. And while it is stated variously in the four letters, in all four instances his prayer was that they might "know" (Eph. 1:15–18; Phil. 1:9–11; Col. 1:9; Philem. 4–6).

It is significant that in all four prayers, the Greek word used for "knowledge" was an intensive word, *epignosis*, instead of the usual *gnosis*. The prefix *epi* serves to lift the idea of knowing beyond that of simply knowing *about*, a superficial acquaintance. *Epi* is used today in speaking of the epicenter of an earthquake—the center of the center. "Epi-knowledge," therefore, is knowing at the center of knowing. In his second great prayer in Ephesians (3:14–19), Paul prayed the paradoxical prayer that they might "know the love . . . that surpasses knowledge." Indeed, the very idea of actually knowing God would be preposterous except for the fact that he makes himself known! He has spoken, and ultimately he spoke the final Word by coming to us in the person of Jesus Christ.

The way the prayer is expressed in Colossians 1 gives an important perspective on the Christian life. Look again at verse

9 where the apostle stated that in his continuous praying for the Colossian church he was constantly asking that God would fill them "with the *knowledge* [*epignosis*] of his will in all spiritual wisdom and understanding." Those are words pertaining to the mind and heart, not to action. But note that in verse 10 he assumed, as a consequence of this knowledge, they would be able "to walk in a manner worthy of the Lord," and then he went on to describe the life that pleases God. In other words, it is the *knowing* (v. 9) that leads to the doing (vv. 10–12).

I'm afraid that for many Christians that order is reversed—it was certainly the case for me. Or perhaps it would be better to say that we are so preoccupied with the *doing* of Christianity that we pay scant attention to the matter of *knowing*. We want to please God, but we assume that it will come about by actions. It is very clear from this passage that when Paul prayed for those Christians, he was praying, first of all, that they would know the Lord. And these prayers were offered on behalf of Christians who already "knew" the Lord.

I hope you are learning with me to dwell continuously on this great theme and to pray constantly the same prayer for ourselves and for those we are called to serve.

For this reason I bow my knees before the Father, from whom every family in heaven and on earth is named, that according to the riches of his glory he may grant you to be strengthened with power through his Spirit in your inner being, so that Christ may dwell in your hearts through faith—that you, being rooted and grounded in love, may have strength to comprehend with all the saints what is the breadth and length and height and depth, and to know the love of Christ that surpasses knowledge, that you may be filled with all the fullness of God. (Eph. 3:14–19)

DAY 18

Knowing Who We Are

Ephesians 1:15–23

For this reason, because I have heard of your faith in the Lord Jesus and your love toward all the saints, I do not cease to give thanks for you, remembering you in my prayers, that the God of our Lord Jesus Christ, the Father of glory, may give you a spirit of wisdom and of revelation in the knowledge of him, having the eyes of your hearts enlightened, that you may know what is the hope to which he has called you, what are the riches of his glorious inheritance in the saints, and what is the immeasurable greatness of his power toward us who believe. (Eph. 1:15–19)

Consider one more prayer for the knowledge of God. In my discovery of the importance of spiritual knowledge, I was drawn to the passage we read today before I discovered that same essential prayer in the other three Prison Epistles. I have grown a great deal since then—in understanding of Scripture, in theological learning, in life experiences and, I trust, in spiritual depth. But at no point in this growth have I had to retract my conviction of the centrality of the concept of the knowledge of God. On the contrary, everything I have studied has been an extension of the discovery that began with Ephesians 1.

Notice that the familiar pattern begins with verse 15. Paul not only stated that he was praying for his readers, but he identified precisely what he prayed for them. His constant prayer was that God, the Father of the Lord Jesus Christ, would "give you a spirit of wisdom and of revelation in the knowledge [epignosis] of him" (v. 17). In this way the eyes of our hearts are enlightened so that we might "know" the hope to which he has called us, the riches that are ours in Christ, and the immeasurably great power that raised Christ from the dead . . . which is the very power that has raised us from spiritual death (1:18–20; 2:1–5). It is essential to note that, in terms of the three ideas of hope, riches, and power, the apostle was not praying that we would have or receive them. He prayed that we would know, since we are "in Christ," that they are already ours.

Now look back to 1:3–14. Those verses are an extraordinary doxology (a word of praise) in which Paul praises the God and Father of our Lord Jesus Christ, "who has blessed us in Christ with every spiritual blessing in the heavenly places" (1:3). He then lists these blessings, starting with the fact that we were chosen (known) from before the creation of the world: "In love he predestined us for adoption . . . through Jesus Christ" (1:4-5). All this was freely given to us through his beloved Son, who has redeemed us through his blood, and through whom God lavished his grace upon us as part of his grand purpose to unite all things under the lordship of Christ. And we were included "in Christ" when we heard the word of truth, the gospel, and having believed, we were sealed in him with the promised Holy Spirit. And all this was "to the praise of his glory" (vv. 6, 12, 14).

Once we comprehend the extent to which God has blessed us in Christ, we are overwhelmed with praise and humility. But that is just our problem—we don't comprehend. We have been adopted into the richest family in the universe and we are constantly lamenting our poverty! When Paul prayed for a spirit of wisdom and revelation, I believe he was praying that we would actually grasp the meaning of the praise he was offering in 1:3–14. It is hard to think of a single portion of Scripture that reveals more of the gracious work of God in salvation than those verses. But they are not simply words; they set forth the spiritual blessings that are already ours in Christ. The prayer is that we would know this in the very core of our being. And knowing in this sense will cause us to live differently, as we noted in the prayer of Colossians 1.

There is one other aspect of our knowledge of God that is evident in this passage. It is that knowing God includes a relationship with each of the persons of the divine Trinity. God the Father has blessed us with every spiritual blessing. He has done this in and through God the Son, and this is communicated to us, and sealed in our hearts, by the ministry of God the Holy Spirit. "Knowing God," therefore, means knowing the Father and the Son and the Holy Spirit. The triune nature of God is never explained in Scripture intellectually or philosophically, but it is revealed in our experience with God as he saves us. In addition to Ephesians 1, look up Ephesians 2:18, 22; 3:14–19; 4:3–5; 2 Thessalonians 2:13–14; and 1 Peter 1:1–2, and mark specific references to the three persons of the Holy Trinity at work in our salvation.[1]

It is therefore our privilege to know communion with God on a level that was not yet made known to Moses, even in the intimacy of his relationship. He prayed for the knowledge of God,

---

1. See my booklet, *What Is True Conversion?* (Phillipsburg, NJ: P&R, 2005), where I explain that our experience of God is the reverse of our usual explanation of him. We first encounter God in the person of the Holy Spirit, who leads us to saving faith in God the Son, through whom we come to know God as our Father.

and God was pleased to answer. But an ever-greater knowledge awaited the coming of his Son, and that knowledge is ours. May God be pleased to give us more and more of "a spirit of wisdom and revelation" to lead us more and more into the knowledge of God (Eph. 1:17).

> For God, who said, "Let light shine out of darkness," has shone in our hearts to give the light of the knowledge of the glory of God in the face of Jesus Christ. (2 Cor. 4:6)

DAY 19

True Sabbath Rest

Hebrews 3:7–4:5

As it is said, "Today, if you hear his voice, do not harden your hearts as in the rebellion." For who were those who heard and yet rebelled? Was it not all those who left Egypt led by Moses? And with whom was he provoked for forty years? Was it not with those who sinned, whose bodies fell in the wilderness? And to whom did he swear that they would not enter his rest, but to those who were disobedient? . . . For we who have believed enter that rest. (Heb. 3:15–18; 4:3)

The Lord said, "My Presence will go with you, and I will give you rest" (Ex. 33:14). Finally, Moses received the blessing he had so doggedly sought. He was able to remove the terrifying prospect of God's sending his people on without him. His patient intercession was rewarded, and it would be the Lord himself who would take them into the Promised Land. But our reading from Hebrews raises the question of a greater rest.

The reference to rest in Exodus 33:14 means the people of Israel dwelling in the land of their fathers, the land promised to them by an oath (see also 33:1; Ps. 95; Heb. 3:16–19). It was to be a place where they would be free from the prospect of slavery, a place to live in peace, and, preeminently, a place where they could meet with the God whose presence was in their midst. Therefore it is called a place of rest. The word *rest* comes into our English language as the word *sabbath*.

Simply a physical resting or a cessation of activity is not the rest, the *Sabbath*, of Scripture. That kind of rest can only be known by being in the presence of God. It is necessary to slow down physically and mentally and to find the place of quiet in order to begin to know rest, but the rest itself is not essentially physical. The Pharisees of Jesus' day had forgotten this point. They thought of the Sabbath as an entity in itself rather than as a God-given mandate to stop one form of activity in order to allow for a quiet time to renew a sense of his presence.

So there can be a *place* of sabbath rest and a time or *day* of sabbath rest. But the deepest form of sabbath rest comes in answer to prayer. Moses regularly went to God in the tent of meeting and spoke with him face-to-face; he was constant in his intercession for the people, and finally he heard the word he was waiting for, "I will give you rest." God gives the real *sabbath*.

The basis for looking beyond the immediate use of the word *rest* in the Lord's response to Moses is the teaching of Hebrews 3 and 4. The writer has in view both the rest of entering the land (3:7–19) and the rest of the seventh day (4:4). However, there is more. He makes it clear that "the promise of entering his rest still stands" (4:1) and that "there remains a Sabbath rest for the people of God" (4:9). Those early forms of Sabbath point to a much more profound *sabbath*. It is a sabbath rest to be found in trusting ourselves to Jesus Christ. *He* is the fulfillment of the Sabbath—not a time or a place, but a Person. "For we who have believed enter that rest" (4:3). Here is yet another example of how the study of Exodus 33 and 34 calls us to center our lives on

Jesus. While Moses may have been anxious about finding the presence of God, we can be sure where it can be found—in the person of our Lord and Savior, our older brother, our high priest, our friend, the Lord Jesus Christ.

But there is a difference between the truth about the sabbath rest and the actual entering into the experience of rest in Christ. In closing, reflect on the hymn that has become my favorite:

> Jesus, I am resting, resting in the joy of what thou art;
> I am finding out the greatness of thy loving heart.
> Thou hast bid me gaze upon thee, as thy beauty fills my soul,
> For by thy transforming power, thou hast made me whole.
>
> O how great thy loving kindness, vaster, broader than the sea!
> O how marvelous thy goodness lavished all on me!
> Yes, I rest in thee, Beloved, know what wealth of grace is thine,
> Know thy certainty of promise, and have made it mine.
>
> Ever lift thy face upon me as I work and wait for thee;
> Resting 'neath thy smile, Lord Jesus, earth's dark shadows flee.
> Brightness of my Father's glory, sunshine of my Father's face,
> Keep me ever trusting, resting, fill me with thy grace.

—JEAN SOPHIA PIGOTT (1876)

DAY 20

Entering the Rest

Hebrews 4:6–13

Since therefore it remains for some to enter it, and those who formerly received the good news failed to enter because of disobedience, again he appoints a certain day, "Today," saying through David so long afterward, in the words already quoted, "Today, if you hear his voice, do not harden your hearts." For if Joshua had given them rest, God would not have spoken of another day later on. So then, there remains a Sabbath rest for the people of God. (Heb. 4:6–9)

"So then, there remains a Sabbath rest for the people of God" (v. 9). The reading from Hebrews makes it very clear that the rest of entering the land was to find a deeper fulfillment in what we can know "today" (vv. 7–8). The word *today* (from Psalm 95) is a reference to the coming of Christ into the world. In that sense, we are living in that same *today* as were those who first read these words from Hebrews. On one level, the writer explains, we enter that rest when we come to faith in Christ (Heb. 4:3). As we have already considered, Jesus is the rest that is promised. But there is another meaning to the word *rest*. Note that the writer goes on to present the idea of Sabbath rest in Christ as an experience that is available for those who "strive to enter that rest" (v. 11). By implication, then, there are some who are trusting in Christ for salvation but are not experiencing the rest that is theirs through him.

This passage defines just what is meant by rest. Look again at verse 10: "for whoever has entered God's rest has also rested from his works as God did from his." There needs to be a point at which we stop insisting that our endeavors are necessary to complete the work of God in our lives. In one sense, we could never have become Christians if we didn't stop working and, by faith, simply receive the gift of salvation. But we still live under the compulsive pull to do our part. Therefore, we do not know the peace—the rest in our spirits—that comes from knowing with certainty that God is truly sovereign and active and that in him we are complete. For most of us that requires the deeper knowledge of the grace of God that comes through time and experience with him.

The initial fulfillment of rest beautifully illustrates the process that is involved. In the spiritual pilgrimage of Israel there were two major crossing points—the Red Sea and the Jordan River. The first crossing, through the Red Sea, was a move from slavery to liberty by means of the power of God and of the blood of the Passover Lamb. God redeemed Israel by grace, just as we are saved by grace through faith.

But although redeemed, God's people did not immediately enter their rest. Instead they entered a period of wilderness, characterized by constant doubts about whether God would stand by his promises. This wilderness period was very important to their spiritual growth as, time and time again, they were given tangible evidence of God's love and his power at work on their behalf. Just as we do, the Israelites needed simple lessons in the goodness of God in the infancy of their experience with him. But the wilderness phase of their spiritual journey was prolonged unnecessarily when they faced a crisis and refused to believe that God was greater than the giants in the land (Num. 13–14; Ps. 95). God was ready to give them rest, but they would not have it on his terms. Consequently, for a whole generation they wandered aimlessly until he brought them again to a time of entering in under the leadership of Joshua.

The second crossing of Israel was the crossing of the Jordan. They moved from the wilderness to rest in the land of promise. This represents the experience of those who already have experienced the grace of salvation, moving from the wilderness of doubt and struggle to a place of knowing the Lord. It is a knowing that allows them to rest in the strength of his presence and promises.

It is important to note that once Israel crossed into the Promised Land, they didn't stop sinning nor did all of their doubts go away. They were finally in the place where God wanted them to be, but life went on with its ups and downs. In the same way, the rest promised in Scripture is not to be thought of as entering some kind of sinless state (or heaven, as pictured in so many gospel songs). When we enter the Sabbath rest, we live our lives for Christ as we always have, with varied successes or failures. But there is a difference—deep within our spirits we know that God really is God and that his love through Jesus is real. It is that knowledge that sustains us, no matter what the circumstances may bring (see Paul's spirit of rest in Phil. 4:11–13).

"Let us strive to enter that rest" (Heb. 4:11). That striving, ironically, is to learn to stop working on our own and to learn more and more of the gracious character of God. This is what God was about to teach Moses.

DAY 21

You Must Go with Us

Exodus 33:12–17; Luke 11:1–13

"For how shall it be known that I have found favor in your sight, I and your people? Is it not in your going with us, so that we are distinct, I and your people, from every other people on the face of the earth?" And the LORD said to Moses, "This very thing that you have spoken I will do, for you have found favor in my sight, and I know you by name." (Ex. 33:16–17)

"And I tell you, ask, and it will be given to you; seek, and you will find; knock, and it will be opened to you. For everyone who asks receives, and the one who seeks finds, and to the one who knocks it will be opened." (Luke 11:9–10)

Every time during the past several years that I have had to face a personal change or a change for the church I was serving as a pastor, I have gone back and prayed these words based on today's passage: "Lord, if your presence doesn't go with us, please don't allow us to make a move, because it is only your presence that makes us different from anyone else." It is so easy to jump at anything new (and in the ministry of the church that usually means something bigger with a greater opportunity to be a witness) without honestly and patiently seeking the face of God. It is frightening to realize that with our slick fund-raising techniques and skill in marketing the church, we know how to make a ministry "successful" whether the Lord is there or not! So we need to pray these words more than ever before.

Notice that Moses offered this prayer after the Lord had just said that his presence would go with him (v. 14). At first, Moses wouldn't take no for an answer; now he seemed to be unwilling to take a yes, or at least to take the answer at face value. It was almost as though he didn't know when to stop asking and to start offering thanks.

But there is another possible explanation: the "you" in verse 14 is singular. It could have a plural sense, but it could also mean that the Lord was still expressing his intention to start over again with Moses as the founder of his chosen people (32:10). In the ESV there is a change in person in verse 15 that reflects a literal reading of the original, "If your presence will not go with me, do not bring us up from here." Perhaps the Lord was promising his presence to all the people by promising it to Moses—but Moses would not take that for granted. In the statements that follow, Moses makes it clear that anything the Lord will do for Moses, he must also do for his people.

Before we find fault with Moses' tenacity (his *impudence*, to use the words of Luke 11:8), note the Lord's response in Exodus 33:17: "This very thing that you have spoken I will do, for you have found favor in my sight, and I know you by name." In addition to knowing him, the Lord says that he was actually pleased with him, and in this setting it means he was pleased with the way Moses prayed.

This is both a confirmation and an illustration of Jesus' teaching about prayer in Luke 11. After teaching his disciples to pray the Lord's Prayer, he told the parable of the persistent friend. Jesus then applied the parable by giving a command to do the kind of determined praying that Moses did. "*Keep on* asking, seeking, knocking" is the sense of the verb in Greek. Then Jesus very emphatically reassured his disciples that this kind of praying is pleasing to God. He used the powerful analogy of the love of human fathers to that of the infinite love of the heavenly Father (vv. 11–13). If we are pleased to hear from our children and love to give them the best that we are able, how much more will that be true of God.

In the light of Moses' prayers for the presence of God with the people, it is worth noting that the "good gift" to be given by the Father, to those who ask, is the Holy Spirit. Surely, of all the things we can and should pray about and for, this request is by far the most significant. In one sense, that prayer was offered by Jesus to the Father, who answered by sending the "Helper, to be with you forever" (John 14:16–18). But we need to pray persistently for a sensitivity to that presence. This is what Paul meant in Ephesians 5:18 when he gave the command, "Be filled with the Spirit." As with Jesus' command to pray in Luke 11:9, this command has an ongoing sense of "be being filled," "keep being filled." It is also the plural—"you together," "you the church, be continuously filled with the presence of the Spirit." After all, as Moses told the Lord, that is what makes a gathering of people distinctly the people of God—God is in their midst. If we lose this, we are no different from any other assembly. We need to pray constantly for a continuous experience of the Spirit's presence and power in our lives and in the churches we are part of. The old saying is true, "You have all of the Holy Spirit, but does the Holy Spirit have all of you?"

DAY 22

Show Me Your Glory

Exodus 33:18–20

Moses said, "Please show me your glory." And he said, "I will make all my goodness pass before you and will proclaim before you my name 'The LORD.' And I will be gracious to whom I will be gracious, and will show mercy on whom I will show mercy. But," he said, "you cannot see my face, for man shall not see me and live." (Ex. 33:18–20)

Moses said, "Please, show me your glory." This request actually to behold God's glory is one of the boldest in all of Scripture. "Glory" in this context refers to a revelation of what theologians call the *essence* of God. That is, whatever it is that makes God *God* is God's glory. Once the tabernacle was actually erected, the Scripture says that "the cloud covered the tent of meeting, and the glory of the LORD filled the tabernacle" (Ex. 40:34). Later in Israel's history, the same expression would be used of the filling of the temple (1 Kings 8:11). This was the purest expression of the majesty of God, and it would dwell between the outstretched wings of the cherubim in the Most Holy Place.

Once a year the high priest was to come into this Most Holy Place with the blood of the lamb to make atonement for the sins of the people. He fully expected to be struck dead if there was anything unacceptable to God (Lev. 16). Isaiah found himself in the presence of this glory, and he fell on his face in terror. He said, "Woe is me! For I am lost . . . for my eyes have seen the King, the LORD of Hosts" (Isa. 6:5). And yet, this is the glory that Moses prayed he might see. Perhaps he didn't fully understand what he was asking for, but I am more inclined to think that he did understand and that his passion to know God was unbounded. He knew he had found favor in God's eyes and he wanted more.

But he was asking for more than God would give. The Lord didn't deny his request, but note in verse 19 that there is a very significant change in what will be revealed. Moses asked to see God's glory, and the Lord said he would cause all his *goodness* to pass in front of him. If "glory" refers to the expression of essence or majesty of God, "goodness" refers to his benefits, the good things he bestows on those he blesses. Those benefits unfold as God proclaims his name (33:19), which he does in 34:5–7. As those verses make clear, God's proclaiming his name means explaining his character—the way he works and the things he does.

This distinction can be very helpful as we try to understand just what it is we are seeking when we pray to know more of God. If it means seeking for the glory of God, then the image in my mind is that of some sort of abstract grasping for light. On the other hand, knowing the goodness of God is something tangible. I can take aspects of that goodness and dwell on them. The psalmist did this in Psalm 103:2: "Bless the LORD, O my soul, and forget not all his benefits," which he then proceeded to list through the rest of the psalm. One medieval mystic wrote of knowing God as the "Cloud of the Unknowing." I have a great deal of respect for the contemplative tradition, but I believe the concept of "cloud" seriously misses the point of our text.

There certainly is an indefinable, unknowable majesty about God. But that is not the aspect of his nature that he has chosen to reveal, either to Moses or to us. He wants us to know his *goodness*. Seeking for what God clearly does not choose to reveal can open the way to some of the forms of thinking and meditation that are characteristic of the various Eastern religions, including the so-called New Age movement. That is why we must let the Scripture restrain as well as direct us in our spiritual pilgrimage.

Actually, it is not quite accurate to say that the Lord would not reveal his glory to Moses. It is better to say that it was not *time* for Moses to see that glory. He certainly experienced a greater measure of glory when he was taken into the very presence of God at death. And in a spectacular manifestation of glory, his prayer was finally answered on the Mount of Transfiguration when he, along with Elijah and three of the disciples, saw Jesus in all of his majesty. Jesus was praying and "his face changed, and his clothes became as bright as a flash of lightning" (Luke 9:28–31 NIV). That is the glory that we, too, will someday know. But it is not time.

The Puritan commentator Matthew Henry added a remark to his discussion of this passage that appears in a source I cannot recall, and it is a fitting word with which to conclude: "In the meantime, let us adore the height of what we do know and the depth of what we do not."

DAY 23

The Cleft of the Rock

Exodus 33:18–23

And the LORD said, "Behold, there is a place by me where you shall stand on the rock, and while my glory passes by I will put you in a cleft of the rock, and I will cover you with my hand until I have passed by. Then I will take away my hand, and you shall see my back, but my face shall not be seen." (Ex. 33:21–23)

The truth of God's sovereignty stands out in the concluding verses of chapter 33. In the next chapter the scene shifts to the mountain, but in the reading for today Moses was still in the tent of meeting that had been pitched on the outskirts of the camp. When the Lord said, "I will be gracious to whom I will be gracious, and will show mercy on whom I will show mercy" (v. 19), he was making it clear that Moses would learn of the goodness of God only because the Lord was pleased to reveal it. Neither Moses nor any of us have any right to know God. In fact, our only "right" is judgment. The apostle Paul quoted this statement in a rigorous defense of the sovereignty of God and concluded, "So then it depends not on human will or exertion, but on God, who has mercy" (Rom. 9:16).

There is much to be said for boldness in prayer and for believing that God is honored when we ask him for great things. But the fact remains that God is God. He is the Almighty Sovereign, Ruler of all of his creation. Although he graciously welcomes us into his presence and condescends in remarkable ways to accommodate our weaknesses, we must never forget who he is.

But God is not aloof or capricious. He is good, and he is merciful. Even though Moses was asking too much when he asked to see God's glory, the Lord was honored by such a bold prayer and provided a way for Moses to take in all that he would choose to reveal of himself. The contrast between God's *glory* and his *goodness* was given to Moses in terms of the difference between seeing the "face" of God, which was not permitted (v. 20), and seeing the "back" or "afterglow" of God (v. 23).

The phrase "cleft of the rock" (v. 22) is a poetic one that excites the imagination. One can picture Moses on the mountain gaining an ever-greater awareness of the approaching majesty. The term *glory* can also be translated *heaviness*. And, as Moses sensed the Lord in his glory coming closer, there must have been that inward sense of pressure that all of us have felt in those "heavy" moments. Then, at just the right time, Moses would have been gently pushed back into a crevice where a rock had split and a shadow would cover his vision. He knew that he was closer to the glory than any mortal had ever known in his earthly existence! The experience of that moment would have been overwhelming—but it was also unique and personal. It is important to note that what was to endure was the spoken word of God ("I . . . will proclaim before you my name" [v. 19]), which Moses was later to write in a book. What has been given to us is not the experience but the Word as a means for us to know God for ourselves.

But in reflecting on the experience of Moses, it is encouraging to note that it was the Lord who provided that opportunity for

Moses to know more of God himself. The Lord said he would direct him to the rock on which he should stand, and "while my glory passes by I will put you in a cleft of the rock, and I will cover you with my hand until I have passed by. Then I will take away my hand, and you shall see my back" (33:22–23). This was the Lord *actively* revealing himself to Moses. It is hard to believe that God will go to such lengths to let us know him. We may acknowledge this truth theologically, and it is certainly evident in the fact of Jesus' coming to be among us. Nevertheless, it is still hard to grasp in a personal way, *but it is true!* "Rock of Ages, cleft for me, let me hide myself in thee."

Lord, I freely acknowledge your sovereignty and bow before you as Lord of all creation. Now give me wisdom and understanding to acknowledge just as freely your willingness to let me know you in all of your goodness.

DAY 24

The Voice of God

Exodus 34:1–5; 1 Kings 19:1–13

The LORD said to Moses, "Cut for yourself two tablets of stone like the first, and I will write on the tablets the words that were on the first tablets, which you broke." . . . The LORD descended in the cloud and stood with him there, and proclaimed the name of the LORD. (Ex. 34:1, 5)

And after the fire the sound of a low whisper. And when Elijah heard it, he wrapped his face in his cloak and went out and stood at the entrance of the cave. And behold, there came a voice to him and said, "What are you doing here, Elijah?" (1 Kings 19:12–13)

We are part of a very experience-centered generation. That experience orientation can look like the search for perfect health, the elevation of self-esteem, "possibility thinking," or the quest for "the spiritual life" with very little concern for defining what is spiritual. But the root of all these varied desires is the need to experience life with relatively little regard for the substance behind the experience. Given the fact that this is the environment in which we are living, we need to recognize how easily we can put our quest to know God into the same sort of framework.

This is why today's reading is critical to our series of meditations. Moses was to prepare to receive that which could be written down. First came the tablets for the Ten Commandments, but there was more. Before he returned to the people, he was told to "write these words" (34:27–28), which would have included all that God said. When we finally come to the actual encounter on the mountain, what Moses was given was not a feeling or some sort of indefinable experience; he was given a word. He heard the voice of God who "proclaimed the name of the LORD" (34:5). This is not to deny that Moses had a profound experience in God's presence. He did, and his face shone as a consequence (34:29). That was deeply personal to Moses. But what endured, to be passed on to future generations, was the written record of the voice of God. The substance behind the experience was the Word of God.

The account of Elijah on this same mountain has striking similarities. After being directed to go to Sinai for a time apart, Elijah traveled "forty days and forty nights to Horeb, the mount of God" (1 Kings 19:8). After a night's rest in a cave, he was told by the Lord to "'go out and stand on the mount before the LORD.' And behold, the LORD passed by" (v. 11). Then came a powerful wind, but that was not where the Lord was to be found. Nor was he in an earthquake or a fire that followed. But finally there came a "low whisper" (I love the King James phrase, a "still small voice"), and Elijah knew that God was present in the voice (v. 12). He covered his face and went out to listen (v. 13). As was true for Moses, the substance of Elijah's experience was the voice—*the Word of God.*

All of this brings us back to the Bible as the basis for our spiritual pilgrimage, if that pilgrimage is to lead us to a true knowledge of God. We must learn to be still and listen for the voice of God. But as we do so, it will come to us from the pages of Scripture and will be brought to living reality through the witness of the Holy Spirit.

DAY 25

Grace or Judgment

Exodus 34:4–7

The LORD passed before him and proclaimed, "The LORD,
the LORD, a God merciful and gracious, slow to anger, and
abounding in steadfast love and faithfulness, keeping steadfast
love for thousands, forgiving iniquity and transgression and sin,
but who will by no means clear the guilty, visiting the iniquity
of the fathers on the children and the children's children, to the
third and the fourth generation." (Ex. 34:6–7)

We have come to the high point of Exodus 32–34. The Lord
actually proclaimed his name to Moses. This means that the
Lord explained or revealed his character to Moses, and through
Moses to us. Martin Luther called this the "sermon on the Name
of God." It was God's answer to Moses' prayer to be shown God's
glory. However, as we have seen, the Lord answered it the way he
saw fit, not necessarily in terms of what Moses expected.

This is the third of the great moments of revelation of God's
name in Exodus. The first revelation of God's name was at the
burning bush (Ex. 3:14–15; 6:2–8), and then there was additional
revelation the first time he wrote down the Ten Commandments

(20:1–6). In the first instance the Lord announced his name and declared that he, as the Lord, would be faithful to the covenant he made with their fathers to deliver his people from bondage. By the time they got to Mount Sinai to receive the Ten, the people had experienced that deliverance, as the Lord reminded them in the first words he spoke from the mountain, "I am the LORD your God, who brought you out of the land of Egypt, out of the house of slavery" (20:2). The emphasis in this second revelation would seem to be on the people's obligation in the covenant relationship. The element of judgment and the Lord's jealousy and justice are very evident in this passage.

But by the time the Lord came to further reveal himself in Exodus 34, the people and Moses had both had significant spiritual experiences. They had witnessed the fearsome majesty of God, they had all actually heard his voice, and they had known the potential for their own depravity. *Now* they were ready to receive a deeper understanding of the nature of the God who had saved and disciplined them.

This illustrates my conviction that, however ardently we may seek for a greater knowledge of God, it will only come at the pace God determines. And it will come in ways such that our experiences will allow us to incorporate the greater revelations meaningfully into our lives. In the case of Moses and the Israelites, it was this time that the Lord chose to explain more fully who he is.

Before we consider the treasury of particular words and phrases, consider the overall message. The Lord emphatically revealed himself, first and foremost, as a God of grace, love, and mercy. Far too often our first instinct is to think of God in terms of his sovereignty and majesty. And when we consider our own sinfulness, we add to that impression the fearful sense of his holiness and judgment. These attributes are certainly true about

God, and they were impressed on the people of Israel as well. But in this passage we have *God himself* telling us what he wants us to know about him, and this is what he says first: "a God merciful and gracious, slow to anger, and abounding in steadfast love and faithfulness, keeping steadfast love for thousands, forgiving iniquity and transgression and sin" (34:6–7). Then he went on to speak of his justice, for that is just as much a part of his name as the mercy. His justice is also part of "all [of his] goodness" (33:19). But it seems evident, from the order in which he revealed his character, that it was his intention that we first of all focus on the fact that he is a gracious and merciful God.

And if that was true for Moses, consider how this wonderful truth has been brought to even greater fulfillment in the coming of Jesus. As we have seen, the covenant name, the LORD, has its highest meaning in the name of Jesus. And because of Jesus, God has a new name. It is "Father." In fact, as children adopted into the household of God, we call him "Abba" (Rom. 8:15; Gal. 4:6), the most intimate word for Father.

Let these next several meditations be times of rejoicing as all of the goodness of God passes in front of us.

> Enter his gates with thanksgiving,
>> and his courts with praise!
>> Give thanks to him; bless his name!
>
> For the LORD is good;
>> his steadfast love endures forever,
>> and his faithfulness to all generations. (Ps. 100:4–5)

God Is Good

Lamentations 3:16–33

"The Lord is my portion," says my soul,
    "therefore I will hope in him."

The Lord is good to those who wait for him,
    to the soul who seeks him.

. . . .

For the Lord will not
    cast off forever,
but, though he cause grief, he will have compassion
    according to the abundance of his steadfast love. (Lam. 3:24–25, 31–32)

"The Lord passed before him and proclaimed, 'The Lord, the Lord, a God merciful and gracious, slow to anger, and abounding in steadfast love and faithfulness, keeping steadfast love for thousands, forgiving iniquity and transgression and sin'" (Ex. 34:6–7). It was an unusually rewarding experience to take the words found in Exodus 34:6–7 and, using the cross-reference part of my study Bible, to trace the themes all over Scripture. This Exodus passage is actually quoted in seven other Old Testament passages (Num. 14:18; Neh. 9:17; Pss. 86:15; 103:7–8; 145:8; Joel 2:13; Jonah 4:2). In the next four meditations we will see how God's people held on to the various aspects of the goodness of God to sustain them in the midst of whatever life had to offer—whether good times or bad times. As you read the suggested Scripture portions, watch for the constant reference to the goodness, or steadfast love, or faithfulness of God. These are not simply abstract ideas, but ways in which a good and merciful God has cared for his people.

One important truth that the Scripture lessons make abundantly clear is that the goodness and graciousness of God do not mean some guarantee of an easy or comfortable life. In fact, it seems that it is out of the ashes of defeat and in times of affliction that the affirmation of the goodness of God is all the sweeter. This thought is basic to a full appreciation of the reading for today.

Jeremiah wrote the book of Lamentations as he walked through the rubble of Jerusalem, the city of God. His entire ministry had been devoted to warning of judgment unless the people turned back to God. But in spite of all of his efforts, that judgment had come and the Babylonian armies had ruined his beloved city. Jeremiah wrote at a time of despair,

> Remember my affliction and my wanderings,
>> the wormwood and the gall!
> My soul continually remembers it
>> and is bowed down within me. (Lam. 3:19–20)

And it is in this setting, not in a time of prosperity, that he recognized his only hope—the truth of the goodness of God.

But this I call to mind,
> and therefore I have hope:

The steadfast love of the Lord never ceases;
> his mercies never come to an end;
they are new every morning;
> great is your faithfulness.

. . . .

For the Lord will not
> cast off forever,
but, though he cause grief, he will have compassion
> according to the abundance of his steadfast love. (3:21–23, 31–32)

Take a moment to recall some period of great difficulty. Perhaps for you it is the present. Although we struggle for explanations, almost invariably deliverance from a sense of despair comes when, like Jeremiah, we rest in the hope of God's love and goodness.

One of the most difficult times that I ever passed through was dealing with the death of my father. God used Psalm 13 to give me a sense of peace, and as I turned to that psalm again and again, I realized that its power was rooted in an affirmation of the goodness of God.

How long, O Lord? Will you forget me forever?
> How long will you hide your face from me?
How long must I take counsel in my soul
> and have sorrow in my heart all the day?
How long shall my enemy be exalted over me?

Consider and answer me, O Lord my God;
> light up my eyes, lest I sleep the sleep of death,

lest my enemy say, "I have prevailed over him,"
    lest my foes rejoice because I am shaken.

But I have trusted in your steadfast love;
    my heart shall rejoice in your salvation.
I will sing to the LORD,
    because he has dealt bountifully with me. (Ps. 13)

DAY 27

God Is Patient

Nehemiah 9:5–37; Exodus 34:6–7

"They refused to obey and were not mindful of the wonders that you performed among them. . . . But you are a God ready to forgive, gracious and merciful, slow to anger and abounding in steadfast love, and did not forsake them. . . . Many years you bore with them and warned them by your Spirit through your prophets. Yet they would not give ear. Therefore you gave them into the hand of the peoples of the lands. Nevertheless, in your great mercies you did not make an end of them or forsake them, for you are a gracious and merciful God." (Neh. 9:17, 30–31)

The LORD passed before him and proclaimed, "The LORD, the LORD, a God merciful and gracious, slow to anger, and abounding in steadfast love and faithfulness, keeping steadfast love for thousands, forgiving iniquity and transgression and sin." (Ex. 34:6–7)

The reading for today takes us to the time of Israel's return from exile in Babylon. Even after the terrible judgment that was described by Jeremiah, the people continued to need godly leaders to bring them to repentance and renewal. In the return from the exile, God used Ezra and Nehemiah for that purpose. The Jews call the priest Ezra the "second Moses." Just as Moses brought order to the people of God after their deliverance from Egypt, so Ezra reorganized the people after their deliverance from Babylon.

The long prayer of confession in today's reading grew out of a time of renewal led by Ezra and Nehemiah. They had gathered the people together and, for an entire day, read to them the Law. "They read from the book, from the Law of God, clearly, and they gave the sense, so that the people understood the reading" (Neh. 8:8). Not surprisingly, the account says that as the people heard the Law read, they began to "mourn and weep" (8:9). But Nehemiah told them to stop weeping and instead to prepare a feast—"Do not be grieved, *for the joy of the Lord* is your strength" (8:10). Nehemiah wanted them to understand that while the Law clearly condemned much of what they had been doing, ultimately their hope rested in the compassionate and merciful nature of God, not on the level of their obedience. This was not to ignore or excuse their sin, for an extensive confession of that sin was prepared and signed (9:38). But woven throughout the confession was a total resting upon the goodness of God.

The aspect of God's goodness that was of particular importance to the people was God's *patience*. To use the time-honored word from the *King James Version*, he is "long-suffering." That is a picturesque word and summarizes the way the Lord dealt with his people over their long history of willfulness and disobedience. "But they and our fathers acted presumptuously and stiffened their neck and did not obey your commandments. They refused to obey and were not mindful of the wonders that you performed among them, but they stiffened their neck and appointed a leader to return to their slavery in Egypt. But you are a God ready to forgive, gracious and merciful, slow to anger and abounding in steadfast love [Note: this is a direct quotation of Exodus 34:6], and did not forsake them" (9:16–17).

And so they moved through their history—"Even when they had made for themselves a golden calf . . . you in your great mercies did not forsake them in the wilderness" (vv. 18–19); "and [they] delighted themselves in your great goodness" (v. 25); "and according to your great mercies you gave them saviors" (v. 27); "you heard from heaven, and many times you delivered them according to your mercies" (v. 28); "nevertheless, in your great mercies you did not make an end of them or forsake them, for you are a gracious and merciful God" (v. 31). Based on this knowledge of their long-suffering God, they prayed for forgiveness to "the great, the mighty, and the awesome God, *who keeps covenant and steadfast love*" (v. 32).

For some reason it is easier to apply this great lesson to others than to our own stories. The Lord could be patient with Israel, but then we wonder how he can put up with our disobedience time after time after time. But just like the people under Ezra, we need to look back and celebrate the fact that it has been God's perseverance, not ours, that has kept us on the path. Our strength, like theirs, is the "joy of the LORD." And in a contemplation of the goodness and patience of God who is "slow to anger," we will be brought to a true place of repentance. All of this brings new meaning to the statement of Paul:

> Or do you presume on the riches of his kindness and forbearance and patience, not knowing that God's kindness is meant to lead you to repentance? (Rom. 2:4)

DAY 28

God Is Loyal

Psalms 107:1–9, 15, 21, 31–32, 43;
118:1–4, 28–29; Exodus 34:6–7

Oh give thanks to the LORD, for he is good,
　　for his steadfast love endures forever!
Let the redeemed of the LORD say so,
　　whom he has redeemed from trouble. (Ps. 107:1–2)

You are my God, and I will give thanks to you;
　　you are my God; I will extol you.
Oh give thanks to the LORD, for he is good;
　　for his steadfast love endures forever! (Ps. 118:28–29)

There is a wonderful aspect of the goodness of God that is celebrated throughout the Scriptures. In Hebrew the word for this is *hesed*, and it has such a rich meaning that it is translated in various ways. The word appears twice in God's revelation to Moses, and in the ESV it is translated "steadfast love"—"abounding in *steadfast love*" and "keeping *steadfast love* for thousands" (Ex. 34:6–7). In the reading for today, the psalmist calls on us to "give thanks to the LORD, for he is good; for his *steadfast love* endures forever!" (Pss. 107:1; 118:1, 29). Later in Psalm 107 the refrain is repeated over and over, "Let them thank the LORD for his *steadfast love*" (vv. 8, 15, 21, 31). Psalm 136 is a litany in which every one of the twenty-six thoughts is answered with "for his *steadfast love* endures forever." In other versions this word is translated as *love*, *lovingkindness*, *mercy*, and *constancy*.

The idea behind *hesed* is a particular kind of love. It is love that produces loyalty. That is why there was no redundancy for the Lord to reveal himself as the God who is both merciful and gracious, the God who is "abounding in steadfast love [*hesed*]." As a way to emphasize the constancy of that love, he added that he keeps or maintains "steadfast love [*hesed*] for thousands." The "thousands" probably refers not just to thousands of individuals, but to "a thousand generations" (Ex. 20:6 NIV). The people of God understood that once he made a promise or commitment, it was contrary to his nature to go back on his word. Love, in this sense, is rooted in the whole idea of his covenant. It is, therefore, integral to the revelation of his covenant name, the LORD.

If a single word must be used, "love" is probably better than "loyalty" because the sense of *hesed* includes the wonderful fact that the Lord *desires* to be in this covenant relationship. He is not simply fulfilling a contract that he would break if he hadn't committed to keeping it, even though there are times when he expresses himself as if that were the case.

Those of us who are married can identify with that feeling. We willingly and joyfully enter into the covenant known as marriage. There grows up a loyalty between a husband and wife that makes the covenant more than just a legally binding contract. But there are occasions when the relationship is strained. At those times, it is the unbreakable nature of the covenant that sustains the marriage until a reconciliation restores the joyful aspect of the loyalty. Magnify the loyalty within the marriage vow to an infinite degree and we begin to understand the depth of God's loyal love, his steadfast love. It is love that endures a thousand generations.

Is it any wonder that of all the characteristics of God's goodness that Israel celebrated, this is perhaps the one they rejoiced in the most? And, as it is with so many of the truths revealed in the Old Testament, the nature of God's steadfast love is brought to an even higher fulfillment in the person and work of Jesus Christ. Consider this word from Hebrews:

> So when God desired to show more convincingly to the heirs of the promise the unchangeable character of his purpose, he guaranteed it with an oath, so that by two unchangeable things, in which it is impossible for God to lie [God's nature and his covenant promise], we who have fled for refuge might have strong encouragement to hold fast to the hope set before us. We have this as a sure and steadfast anchor of the soul, a hope that enters into the inner place behind the curtain, where Jesus has gone as a forerunner on our behalf. (Heb. 6:17–20)

> I will extol you, my God and King,
>   and bless your name forever and ever.
> Every day I will bless you
>   and praise your name forever and ever.
>
> . . . .
>
> The Lord is gracious and merciful,
>   slow to anger and abounding in steadfast love.
> The Lord is good to all,
>   and his mercy is over all that he has made. (Ps. 145:1–2, 8–9)

DAY 29

Forgiveness of Sin

Psalm 103; Exodus 34:6–7

Bless the Lord, O my soul,
　and all that is within me,
　bless his holy name!
Bless the Lord, O my soul,
　and forget not all his benefits,
who forgives all your iniquity,
　who heals all your diseases,
who redeems your life from the pit,
　who crowns you with steadfast love and mercy.

. . . .

For as high as the heavens are above the earth,
　so great is his steadfast love toward those who fear him;
as far as the east is from the west,
　so far does he remove our transgressions from us. (Ps.
103:1–4, 11–12)

The psalm of David that we read today is one of the favorites
of the people of God. We are called to praise the Lord from the

very depths of our souls. One of the most important ways to give praise to our wonderful God is to "forget not all his benefits" (v. 2). David recited a list of the benefits that have come to us from the Lord who is "merciful and gracious, slow to anger and abounding in steadfast love [love, mercy, lovingkindness, covenant loyalty—*hesed*]" (v. 8). Remarkably, Exodus 34:6 is quoted yet another time.

Of all the benefits listed, the one David celebrated most passionately was the forgiveness of sin. It was not only the first benefit he mentioned (v. 3), but he returned to it after the citation of Exodus 34:6. The Lord's slowness to anger means that "he does not deal with us according to our sins, nor repay us according to our iniquities" (v. 10). Furthermore, "as far as the east is from the west, so far does he remove our transgressions from us" (v. 12), and like a compassionate father toward his children, so the Lord "shows compassion" (v. 13) and "remembers that we are dust" (v. 14). He understands our weakness and the depth of our rebellion far better than we do. Try to let your mind linger on those wonderful words. Perhaps we have come to take them for granted.

David certainly didn't take for granted the forgiveness of sin. On many occasions he had sought forgiveness but none more ardently than after his sin with Bathsheba came to light.

Have mercy on me, O God,
    according to your steadfast love [*hesed*];
according to your abundant mercy
    blot out my transgressions.
Wash me thoroughly from my iniquity,
    and cleanse me from my sin! (Ps. 51:1–2)

Nor would the children of Israel have taken for granted forgiveness of sin. We need to remember the context of the passage in

Exodus. The people had defied everything that God had told them. To be sure, they were judged for their sin (we will consider the matter of justice next), but Moses was being told that once the sin had been dealt with, *it was over*. With an emphatic statement, the Lord said that he would forgive "iniquity and transgression and sin" (Ex. 34:7), a description of the very things that had just gone on in the camp.

And of all people, we cannot take for granted the forgiveness of sin. We stand before God cleansed and welcomed with the same depth of compassion with which the prodigal son was welcomed home. If ever we are tempted to think of that as a minor "benefit," all we need to do is stop and consider the price that was paid. Think of our Lord Jesus on the cross. "For our sake he made him to be sin who knew no sin, so that in him we might become the righteousness of God" (2 Cor. 5:21). "In him we have redemption through his blood, the forgiveness of our trespasses, according to the riches of his grace" (Eph. 1:7).

Is this more than a doctrinal concept for you? Do you truly know yourself to be forgiven through the merits of Christ? I know that this is a serious struggle for many who love the Lord. After living this long in the faith, we should be more victorious over our flesh. But then we need to reflect not only on the work of Christ but also to remember that God knows far more of our "wickedness, rebellion, and sin" than we ever will—and he is the one who declares us forgiven. This is why the communion is called the "Eucharist"—the thanksgiving. We must come again and again to celebrate this mercy of God.

> Blessed is the one whose transgression is forgiven,
>   whose sin is covered.
> Blessed is the man against whom the LORD counts no iniquity,
>   and in whose spirit there is no deceit.

For when I kept silent, my bones wasted away
  through my groaning all day long.
For day and night your hand was heavy upon me;
  my strength was dried up as by the heat of summer.

I acknowledged my sin to you,
  and I did not cover my iniquity;
I said, "I will confess my transgressions to the LORD,"
  and you forgave the iniquity of my sin. (Ps. 32:1–5, a psalm of David)

DAY 30

God Is Just

Exodus 34:4–7; 20:1–6

So Moses cut two tablets of stone like the first. And he rose
early in the morning and went up on Mount Sinai, as the LORD
had commanded him, and took in his hand two tablets of stone.
The LORD descended in the cloud and stood with him there,
and proclaimed the name of the LORD. The LORD passed before
him and proclaimed, "The LORD, the LORD, a God merciful and
gracious, slow to anger, and abounding in steadfast love and
faithfulness, keeping steadfast love for thousands, forgiving
iniquity and transgression and sin, but who will by no means
clear the guilty, visiting the iniquity of the fathers on the children and the children's children, to the third and the fourth generation." (Ex. 34:4–7)

As the revelation of God's name moves to the issue of
"punishing the guilty," it is tempting to think that we have
completed the unveiling of the goodness of God, which has
been the theme of the last several meditations. But this cannot
be so. The Lord said to Moses that in proclaiming his name
to him, he would "make *all* [his] goodness pass before [him]"

(33:19). The justice of God is an aspect of his goodness. It is absolutely essential to the working of the universe God created and pronounced "very good" (Gen. 1:31). What kind of world would this be if there were no standards, no right and wrong? (We are rapidly finding out!) It is our gracious and merciful God who has established and declared those standards. The fact that he holds the world to those standards is the essence of justice. Another of the "benefits" for which we give praise to God is that "the LORD works righteousness and justice for all who are oppressed" (Ps. 103:6). Our good God is righteous and administers justice. He "will by no means clear the guilty" (Ex. 34:7).

It is striking, however, to note the difference in the way the Lord spoke the first time he gave the Ten Commandments (Ex. 20) and the way he made himself known as he prepared to give them a second time. There is a reversal in the order of judgment and grace (see also 20:5–6 and 34:6–7). As we have already noted, the revelation of chapter 34 came out of an experience of both judgment and grace. Many commentators suggest that this kind of experience meant that Israel was ready to hear the message of grace and compassion—without taking it as a *carte blanche* to do anything they wanted.

I believe most of us pass through a similar stage of growth as we begin to understand more of the nature of God (at least this was true for me). In the most initial phases of our spiritual lives, we are filled with the joy of forgiveness and the privilege of being a child of God. But then as we get more serious about actually living out our faith, we come face-to-face with the depth of our sinfulness. We know we are forgiven, but we become convinced that we must overcome the flesh in order to please God. Not only are we dealing with our weakness, but as we read the Scriptures in a more disciplined way, we also begin to see more and more of the majesty, holiness, and sovereignty of God. If God is so mysterious and almighty but is also just in his dealing with me, then who am I?

That is a very uncomfortable place to be, but at the same time I believe it is quite necessary for our growth. We, too, need to come to the mountain of God, as it smokes and belches fire, and recognize that our God is the Almighty. He is Lord of all creation and in his infinite justice he does not ignore those who rebel against him. Here is the place for the fear of God (Ex. 20:20). In our feel-good evangelical world, the unwillingness of many to faithfully proclaim God as holy and just not only tends to trivialize God, but it also keeps people at a level of spiritual immaturity. They are happy only with a God who makes them feel comfortable—and that is not the God who reveals himself in the Scriptures.

Once we have gotten *that* message, however, I believe it is then time to hear the word of grace from Exodus 34. That is how God himself wants us to know him—when we are ready to receive this word. For those of us living under the new covenant, I think this is particularly important. It is not that God has reversed justice and grace, but justice has been *fulfilled* in Jesus' death on the cross. In Jesus we have come into the fullness of what God created us to be. Therefore, it is time to enjoy our freedom, not cower under the demands of the Law.

Reflect on these words of the apostle Paul from the eighth chapter of Romans. They come immediately after he spoke of the agony of spirit that resulted when he held his life up to the demands of the Law (7:15–23).

There is therefore now no condemnation for those who are in Christ Jesus. For the law of the Spirit of life has set you free in Christ Jesus from the law of sin and death. For God has done what the law, weakened by the flesh, could not do. By sending his own Son in the likeness of sinful flesh and for sin, he condemned sin in the flesh, in order that the righteous requirement of the law might be fulfilled in us, who walk not according to the flesh but according to the Spirit. (Rom. 8:1–4)

DAY 31

The Sins of the Fathers

Numbers 14:17–35

"The LORD is slow to anger and abounding in steadfast love, forgiving iniquity and transgression, but he will by no means clear
the guilty, visiting the iniquity of the fathers on the children, to
the third and the fourth generation." . . . Then the LORD said,
"I have pardoned, according to your word. But truly, as I live . . .
none of the men who have seen my glory and my signs that I
did in Egypt and in the wilderness, and yet have put me to the
test these ten times and have not obeyed my voice, shall see the
land that I swore to give to their fathers." (Num. 14:18, 20–23)

The last phrase to consider in the Lord's proclamation of his
name to Moses is the haunting phrase, "visiting the iniquity of
the fathers on the children, to the third and the fourth generation" (Num. 14:18). This was repeated from the first giving of
the commandments (Ex. 20:5). It is cited again in Numbers 14:18
and in Jeremiah 32:18 (where it is paraphrased, "you repay the
guilt of fathers to their children after them"). The words have
long captured the attention of literary people, and the expression
"sins of the fathers" can be found as a title for novels and plays.

What could this mean? Is the Lord saying that his anger over sin cannot be satisfied unless four generations feel his judgment? Is this what he means when he says he is a "jealous God" (Ex. 20:5; 34:14)? Doesn't this contradict the teaching that every person is accountable for his or her sins? For a long time I have wrestled with the meaning of that statement. And it is my strong conviction that far from revealing a capriciousness in the character of God, it is essentially a revelation about the character of sin. We tend to treat sin too casually, as though it applies only to the moment and has few, if any, consequences. In the frightening words of this verse, our gracious and compassionate God is trying to tell us that sin *does* have serious consequences. And in many cases, those consequences will pass from generation to generation.

The reading today is an excellent illustration of this principle at work. The context of Numbers 14 is the report of the spies who scouted out the Promised Land. The great majority of the people rejected Joshua and Caleb and believed those spies who were convinced that it would be impossible to overcome the people of great heights ("giants" KJV) and their fortified cities (Num. 13:26–33). Not only was this a failure of nerve, but also it was the last straw in the people's unwillingness to trust God. This time, even when Moses claimed the Lord's Exodus 34 promise of forgiveness (Num. 14:17–20) and the Lord did forgive them, there were serious consequences. The rebellion of the Israelites caused the Lord to declare that the entire generation would die off before he would bring his people into the land (Num. 14:21–23). What is significant for this lesson is the statement in 14:33 that not only would the rebellious people die for their sin, but also "*your children* shall be shepherds in the wilderness forty years and shall suffer *for your faithlessness.*" In the very nature of the situation, the children would be forced to share in the suffering that was a consequence of their parents' sin. This is life, and it is important that we recognize it.

The world seems to have a better handle on this biblical principle than many believers do. It is not an overstatement to say that much of modern psychology is founded on a serious regard for the "sins of the fathers." In many respects it has perverted the concept, but that doesn't deny the importance of looking back for generations to understand how the sins of the fathers have emotionally or even physically handicapped the children, who in turn pass them on to their children. It is becoming clear, for example, that the great majority of those who abuse children were themselves abused. And consider the important research that has been done on the consequences of parents' alcoholism on children.

In my experience with counseling couples who are about to marry, I have learned to take a great deal of time to talk through the home environments in which the prospective partners grew up. In the conversation, I commonly hear that the problems experienced in his or her home were experienced also in the homes of their grandparents (the "third generation"). My objective in this exercise is not to offer some kind of prescription about what kind of marriage they will have based on how their forefathers' actions have cursed (or blessed) them. Rather, it is to gain a realistic understanding of the "sins of the fathers." That way the couple can know, in more specific ways, how to pray for, and apply, grace.

The "sins of the fathers" is a statement of law. That is, it is the Lord telling us the nature of the world as he created it. When we defy that created order, we will suffer consequences and, tragically, so will our children. But that is not to say this is how it *must* be. We have trusted God to graciously remove the most serious consequence of our sin—judgment. We should, therefore, also trust him to graciously break that terrible chain of one generation bringing a curse on the next. We often say, "By God's grace I will . . ." That should not be a casual statement. To invoke the grace of God is probably the most important thing we can do to see changes in our lives.

> But he said to me, "My grace is sufficient for you, for my power is made perfect in weakness." Therefore I will boast all the more gladly of my weaknesses, so that the power of Christ may rest upon me. (2 Cor. 12:9)

DAY 32

Moses Worshiped

Exodus 34:8–9

And Moses quickly bowed his head toward the earth and worshiped. And he said, "If now I have found favor in your sight, O Lord, please let the Lord go in the midst of us, for it is a stiff-necked people, and pardon our iniquity and our sin, and take us for your inheritance." (Ex. 34:8–9)

"And Moses quickly bowed his head toward the earth and worshiped." What else could he have done? He was in the cleft of the rock with only the shadow of God's hand shielding him from the very essence of God's glory. His prayer to be shown God's glory was answered as much as it could be in mortal existence. He was coming to know the Lord in all his goodness. I don't think Moses had to deliberately plan some sort of response. There could be only one thing to do at this sacred moment—he bowed low and worshiped!

When Elijah heard the voice of God on this same mountain, "he wrapped his face in his cloak and went out and stood at the entrance of the cave" (1 Kings 19:13). When Job finally met God after crying out for a hearing, he worshiped. "I had heard of you by the hearing of the ear, but now my eye sees you; therefore I despise myself, and repent in dust and ashes" (Job 42:5–6). Isaiah could only fall on his face in humility in the presence of the glory of God (Isa. 6:1–5). The wise men, on entering the house and seeing the child Jesus, "fell down and worshiped him" (Matt. 2:11). When Thomas finally met the risen Christ, he could only worship and say, "My Lord and my God!" (John 20:28). When John saw the glorified Christ on the island of Patmos, he said, "I fell at his feet as though dead" (Rev. 1:17). And the picture of heaven that is opened to us throughout Revelation is that of continuous worship: "Day and night they never cease to say, 'Holy, holy, holy, is the Lord God Almighty, who was and is and is to come!'" (4:8). "The twenty-four elders fall down before him who is seated on the throne and worship him who lives forever and ever" (4:10). "And the four living creatures said, 'Amen!' and the elders fell down and worshiped" (5:14).

From these examples in Scripture, it would seem that while there is singing and praise and expressions of repentance, the most essential element of worship is silence and humble submission. We are told in Psalm 46:10, "Be still, and know that I am God." That thought should encourage us because although it is hard, it is something we can do. Our worship may not always come as a result of a dramatic encounter. In fact, that will rarely be the case; but learning to be still in the presence of God puts us in the same place as the great worshipers of Scripture. Jesus taught that our Father is actually seeking for true worshipers, those who worship "in spirit and truth" (John 4:23–24).

Henri Nouwen has a great deal to say about the importance of learning to be quiet before God. He says, "This asks for much discipline and risk taking because we always seem to have something more urgent to do and 'just sitting there' and 'doing nothing' often disturbs us more than it helps. But there is no way around this. Being useless and silent in the presence of our God belongs to the core of all prayer."[1]

Lord, help me to learn to be still and to know that you are God!

1. Henri Nouwen, *Reaching Out: The Three Movements of the Spiritual Life* (New York: Doubleday, 1975), 97.

DAY 33

Covenant Renewal

Exodus 34:8–11; Jeremiah 31:31–34

And Moses quickly bowed his head toward the earth and worshiped. And he said, "If now I have found favor in your sight, O Lord, please let the Lord go in the midst of us, for it is a stiff-necked people, and pardon our iniquity and our sin, and take us for your inheritance." And he said, "Behold, I am making a covenant. Before all your people I will do marvels, such as have not been created in all the earth or in any nation. And all the people among whom you are shall see the work of the LORD, for it is an awesome thing that I will do with you. Observe what I command you this day. Behold, I will drive out before you the Amorites, the Canaanites, the Hittites, the Perizzites, the Hivites, and the Jebusites." (Ex. 34:8–11)

"Behold, the days are coming, declares the LORD, when I will make a new covenant with the house of Israel and the house of Judah." (Jer. 31:31)

Without question, Moses was personally fulfilled through his meeting with God. What more could any human being ask than to have such an encounter? But that wasn't enough for Moses, as we learn from the first part of today's reading. He was also called to be a leader and, therefore, even in his worship, he sought once again to be assured of the presence of the Lord with the people. Acknowledging what the Lord had already said about the people (that they were "stiff-necked," [Ex. 33:5]), Moses also quoted the very words the Lord had just used (34:7) and asked pardon for their iniquity and their sin. In what was probably a reference to the Lord's words before the first giving of the Ten (19:5), Moses laid claim to Israel's being God's "inheritance" (34:9).

The answer Moses received was more than he or the people had any right to expect. In the earlier promise, the Lord had said, "Now therefore, if you will indeed obey my voice and keep my covenant, you shall be my treasured possession among all peoples" (19:5). Israel had neither obeyed God's voice nor kept the covenant—they had not even come close! But in a declaration that was totally consistent with his gracious nature and his great plan of redemption, the Lord said he was "making a covenant" with them (34:10). Actually, this would be a renewal of the covenant made when Moses went up to the mountain the first time. The various laws that followed can all be found in chapters 21–23.

To appreciate the significance of this moment it is helpful to note that the literal translation of the phrase "make a covenant" in 34:10 is "*cut* a covenant." (This is true for other places where the term appears, as well.) That meant that the Lord was once again prepared to go beyond merely promising to be their God—he would seal that promise with blood! (Ex. 24:1–8 was the actual covenant ceremony.) The blood oath was a common form of establishing covenants or treaties in the ancient world. Often people would cut themselves to seal their commitment to their gods. But in this instance it was the Lord *himself* who did the cutting; it was a sign that he would absolutely stand behind the commitments he had made to his people. The idea of *hesed* love is rooted in God's willingness to make covenants in spite of, not because of, the response of his people. The Lord went on to say that his covenanted commitment to them would cause him to "do marvels, such as have not been created in all the earth or in any nation. And all the people among whom you are shall see the work of the LORD, for it is an awesome thing that I will do with you" (34:10; see also Deut. 4:32–40).

The God who reveals himself in Scripture is a covenant-making and a covenant-keeping God. For many of us who come to faith in Christ with little or no biblical background, faith is a matter of *our* commitment. We "accept Jesus as our personal Savior," or words to that effect. This is something we have decided to do. While that is true on one level, there is a foundation under our commitment—it is God's covenant. Underneath my acceptance of Jesus is an eternal covenant, sealed by blood, through which God willed to save me.

As is very clear in today's reading from Jeremiah 31, the covenant was not just part of the Old Testament; it was the framework through which God would save the world. The numerous New Testament references to this passage (Hebrews 8 in particular) make it clear that when the Lord spoke of making a new covenant with Judah and Israel, he meant a covenant with the *whole* people of God, not the Hebrew nation in a purely physical sense. "People" now includes those of all races. When Jesus instituted the communion supper, he said, "This is my blood of *the covenant* [modern translations do not have the word *new* before "covenant"], which is poured out for many for the forgiveness of sins" (Matt. 26:28). The book of Hebrews ends with the benediction, "Now may the God of peace who brought again from the dead our Lord Jesus, the great shepherd of the sheep, by the blood of *the eternal covenant . . .*" (13:20). Ultimately, there is not an old or a new covenant, but *the* covenant that God has sealed through the blood of his own Son. This is the foundation of our eternal salvation.

A debtor to mercy alone, of covenant mercy I sing;
Nor fear, with Thy righteousness on, my person and off'ring to
    bring.
The terrors of law and of God with me can have nothing to do;
My Savior's obedience and blood hide all my transgressions
    from view.

The work which His goodness began, the arm of His strength
    will complete;
His promise is Yea and Amen, and never was forfeited yet.
Things future, nor things that are now, nor things below or
    above,
Can make Him His purpose forgo, or sever my soul from His
    love.

—AUGUSTUS M. TOPLADY (1771)

DAY 34

Covenant Rules

Exodus 34:10–26

"Take care, lest you make a covenant with the inhabitants of the land to which you go, lest it become a snare in your midst. You shall tear down their altars and break their pillars and cut down their Asherim (for you shall worship no other god, for the Lord, whose name is Jealous, is a jealous God), lest you make a covenant with the inhabitants of the land, and when they whore after their gods and sacrifice to their gods and you are invited, you eat of his sacrifice, and you take of their daughters for your sons, and their daughters whore after their gods and make your sons whore after their gods." (Ex. 34:12–16)

It would be tempting to set aside these verses we read today as having no meaning for our studies. But, as usually happens, a more careful reflection will make us think otherwise. The specific laws (an expanded version can be found in Exodus 21–23) certainly pertain to Israel in its unique setting. But considered in the context of the renewal of the covenant, there are some very important lessons.

In studies of the Lord's willingness to enter into covenants with his people, most theologians are careful to point out that God's covenants are unilateral, not bilateral. That means that when God makes, or cuts, a covenant, it is not negotiated in the way we would think of in a contract—each party has an obligation, and the contract is void if either party does not measure up. Rather, it is a commitment the Lord makes and keeps, and its fulfillment is dependent on his power. Ultimately then, the hope of Israel, as well as our hope, rests in the power and mercy of God, not in our obedience or in keeping our part of the bargain.

However, this resting in the strength and mercy of the Lord should not obscure the important truth that God always expects a response to his giving of the covenant. By faith, we believe in the truth of God's promise, and in thankfulness for his grace, we pledge our obedience. That pattern holds whether we are living under the old or new covenant. In the reading for today, there was a clear call for Israel to separate from those things that would pull them away from the Lord. They were also to build disciplines into their daily lives that would continually renew their faith. That is totally consistent with the teaching of the New Testament to "put off your old self" and "put on the new self" (Eph. 4:22–24; Col. 3:9).

In the first place, there needed to be a willingness to be separate from the world (34:12–17). Twice the Lord commanded his people not to enter treaties or covenants with the unbelieving and pagan peoples that would be around them. Of particular concern was the covenant of marriage (v. 16). God's stipulation was not to keep Israel from *associating* with other nations, but it was a prohibition against actually *participating* in their false worship. That is where formal treaties would inevitably lead. Through his covenant, the Lord had pledged his loyalty to his people, and he expected the same of them. That is the sense in which he is "jealous" (v. 14). These commands to remain separate were tied directly to obedience to the first two commandments (vv. 14, 17). Clearly, a willingness to step away from surrounding paganism is at the core of the obedient life. In a letter to new Christians who were unsure of their faith, the apostle John said: "Do not love the world or the things in the world. If anyone loves the world, the love of the Father is not in him" (1 John 2:15).

In addition to the matter of separation from the world, there is a second overall emphasis. Our reading makes it clear that obedience to the covenant called for a discipline of ordering life in a way that allowed a continuous focus on God and his goodness (Ex. 34:18–26). The weekly and annual cycle of feasts and offerings served as a wonderful means of filling up the personal and family life of Israel with times of worship and remembrance. The Lord was careful to show that separation *from* the world was not an end in itself. But it would allow his people to be separated *unto* him so that they could enjoy the delights of being God's own "treasured possession" (19:5). We miss out on the actual enjoyment of God because we have so much "junk" in our lives. As we have seen already, such separation is the essence of Sabbath rest.

Knowing God and obeying God are not separate issues. To know God in the sense that we have been studying means that we will respond sincerely to the God of our salvation and say, "All that the Lord has spoken we will do" (19:8; 24:3). That will drive us to Christ, who alone can truly obey, but a new life in Christ gives us a desire to obey.

He is the propitiation for our sins, and not for ours only but also for the sins of the whole world. And by this we know that we have come to know him, if we keep his commandments. Whoever says "I know him" but does not keep his commandments is a liar, and the truth is not in him, but whoever keeps his word, in him truly the love of God is perfected. By this we may know that we are in him: whoever says he abides in him ought to walk in the same way in which he walked. (1 John 2:2–6)

DAY 35

Write It Down

Exodus 34:27–28;
Deuteronomy 31:7–13, 23–27

And the LORD said to Moses, "Write these words, for in accordance with these words I have made a covenant with you and with Israel." (Ex. 34:27)

When Moses had finished writing the words of this law in a book to the very end, Moses commanded the Levites who carried the ark of the covenant of the LORD, "Take this Book of the Law and put it by the side of the ark of the covenant of the LORD your God, that it may be there for a witness against you." (Deut. 31:24–26)

Both of today's readings make it clear that God's intention was not only to speak to the Israelites, but also that his words actually be written down so that they can be read and understood and passed along to future generations. We are rightfully called "the people of the book," and that book is the Bible.

Have you noticed that the phrase *Holy Bible* has disappeared from the front covers of many newer editions of Scripture (the

ESV is a happy exception!)? Instead, what we typically find is the name of the particular translation, or brand, of Bible. That discovery filled me with real sadness, because it is hard to think of a more apt word for the Bible than "holy." I hope it doesn't suggest that we who gladly accept the label "Bible-believing Christian" have lost a sense of reverence for the Book even as we strive to make it more and more useful.

As a book, the Bible is paper and ink like any other book. However, the words that are presented to our eyes—not just the substance, but the *very words*—are the words that the Lord directed Moses and the other human authors to write down. Those words have been lovingly written, copied, preserved, translated, and passed from generation to generation. Because of this gift, we have been able to read and enter into the actual encounter of the Lord God with the man Moses.

God instructed, "Write these words" (Ex. 34:27). This seems to be the first specific directive to do so. (Of course, God himself began the process by writing down the Ten Commandments.) It is entirely possible that the actual written Scripture began at this point. Exodus was probably the first book to be fully written out, and sometime in the years before his death, we can assume Moses wrote Genesis as well as the other three "Books of Moses," as they are called. Moses was writing up until the day of his death, as is evident from Deuteronomy 31:11–13, where Moses directed that the people be assembled to hear the reading of the Law. It was through reading what had been written down and preserved that God's will could be made known to the children and to all succeeding generations. This established the pattern by which God would make his truth known.

When Moses died, it was as though his "holy" pen was passed to prophets and poets and teachers who continued to put into writing the words of God. As Peter explained, "Men spoke from God as they were carried along by the Holy Spirit" (2 Peter 1:21). Paul called the Scriptures "breathed out by God" (2 Tim. 3:16), placing the written Word on the same level as the very breath that created the universe. Jesus himself built virtually everything he taught and did on the words of Scripture. He then promised the Holy Spirit to enable the apostles to recall and accurately record his words (John 16:12–15). The elders of the early church prayed, "Sovereign Lord . . . who through the mouth of our father David, your servant, said by the Holy Spirit . . ." and then they quoted from Psalm 2 (Acts 4:24–25). That may be the most concise explanation of the inspiration of Scripture to be found. God spoke by *the Holy Spirit*, through *the mouth* of his human servants, *and it was written down* and preserved.

Examples can be multiplied to serve as a reminder that we indeed have a *holy* Bible. But now it is our responsibility and privilege to open this treasure and let it speak. Come to the Bible with reverence—but come! This is not a buried treasure or museum of the past. The Bible lives because God, whose very nature it is to communicate, lives. Read again from A. W. Tozer:

> The Bible is the inevitable outcome of God's continuous speech. It is the infallible declaration of His mind for us, put into our familiar human words. I think a new world will arise out of the religious mists when we approach our Bible with the idea that it is not only a book which was once spoken, but a book which is *now speaking*. The prophets habitually said, "Thus *saith* the Lord." They meant their hearers to understand that God's speaking is in the continuous present.
>
> If you would follow on to know the Lord, come at once to the open Bible expecting it to speak to you. Do not come with

the notion that it is a thing that you may push around at your convenience. It is more than a thing, it is a voice, a word, the very Word of the living God.[1]

1. A. W. Tozer, *The Pursuit of God* (Camp Hill, PA: Christian Publications, 1982), 82–83.

Moses' Shining Face

Exodus 34:29–35

When Moses came down from Mount Sinai, with the two tablets of the testimony in his hand as he came down from the mountain, Moses did not know that the skin of his face shone because he had been talking with God. Aaron and all the people of Israel saw Moses, and behold, the skin of his face shone, and they were afraid to come near him. But Moses called to them, and Aaron and all the leaders of the congregation returned to him, and Moses talked with them. (Ex. 34:29–31)

The passage we have been studying began with Moses' coming down from Sinai to find an orgy of idolatry and sensuality. As it concludes, Moses again returns to the people after forty days on the mountain. This time they were waiting to receive what he would bring them from the Lord their God. It is a quiet and fitting end to the study of this remarkable encounter.

As he returned to the camp, he brought two things with him. In his *hands*, he brought the Ten Commandments. Significantly, they are called here, as well as in several other places, "the testimony" (Ex. 16:34; 31:18; 32:15). God bears witness to his person and will through the written Word. But secondly, on his *face* Moses brought a small taste of the glory that he had been experiencing. Moses was unaware of this second gift, but the people immediately knew it and felt afraid.

The word translated "shone" (the NIV uses the word *radiant*) is not the usual word for an external or physical shining (in Ps. 69:31 it means *horn*). It may point to the fact that the radiance coming from Moses was not primarily something *seen* as it was something *sensed* by those in his presence. Without consciously trying to do so, he was reflecting to the people something of "all the goodness" of God. His time with God had changed him. Notice from the passage that Moses immediately reassured the people, and they came back to him (v. 31).

My initial reading of this incident left me with the mental picture of Moses walking around the camp wearing a veil while people avoided him. But the passage makes it clear that Moses would remove the veil during the times he taught the people the Word of God (vv. 32–33). So a more accurate picture is that of people who were initially awestruck, eagerly crowding around Moses whenever he would teach them. The combination of the authoritative word and the reflection of the majesty of God in Moses' face must have been irresistible. And when they would ask Moses to tell them more about God, the reality behind his words could have been felt as well as heard. The people in that camp could have used the words spoken by the two disciples who met Jesus on the road to Emmaus: "Did not our hearts burn within us while he talked to us on the road, while he opened to us the Scriptures?" (Luke 24:32).

As a pastor and preacher, my personal definition of effective preaching has been taken from that beautiful meeting in Luke 24. It has been my desire to have the enabling to open the Scriptures in such a way that people would encounter the risen Christ and know the "burning of the heart." However, I am *not* the risen Christ, and therefore this incident in Exodus 34 may be a better model to consider. Moses, too, was a sinful person. But before he brought the people the Word of God, he had spent enough time in the presence of God that something of that presence rubbed off as he taught. Furthermore, we read that Moses regularly returned to the presence of God so that the radiance was constantly being renewed (vv. 34–35). The opportunity to spend forty days on a mountain with God is a rare privilege, but a "tent of meeting"—a prayer closet—is always available.

Those same realities—the written Word and the presence of the living God—are with us now when a man of God opens the Bible to preach. Both are critically important. The Word without the reality of God is sterile; a sense of God's presence without the Word to explain it can be an undefined spirituality. But when the two come together there is teaching that moves the soul.

Glorious Father, we pray for those called to the ministry of teaching and preaching your holy Word. Grant that they may never give forth that Word without also sharing some measure of the glory they have experienced in your presence. As you did for Moses, give them the desire and the determination to wait before you on behalf of the people you have called them to lead.

DAY 37

The Radiance of God's Glory

2 Corinthians 3:7–18; Hebrews 1:1–3

Now if the ministry of death, carved in letters on stone, came with such glory that the Israelites could not gaze at Moses' face because of its glory, which was being brought to an end, will not the ministry of the Spirit have even more glory? . . . Since we have such a hope, we are very bold, not like Moses, who would put a veil over his face so that the Israelites might not gaze at the outcome of what was being brought to an end. But their minds were hardened. For to this day, when they read the old covenant, that same veil remains unlifted, because only through Christ is it taken away. Yes, to this day whenever Moses is read a veil lies over their hearts. But when one turns to the Lord, the veil is removed. Now the Lord is the Spirit, and where the Spirit of the Lord is, there is freedom. (2 Cor. 3:7–8, 12–17)

As we noted in the meditation for Day 2, the encounter between Moses and the Lord, glorious as that was, has an even greater fulfillment. In 2 Corinthians 3 and 4, the apostle Paul uses the imagery of the veil over Moses' face to explain the privileges that belong to those who live under the new covenant (3:6), which he also calls "the ministry of the Spirit" (3:8). The concluding meditations will focus on this New Testament commentary on Moses' experience and the application that the apostle makes to our own experience in Christ.

It is striking to note Paul's preoccupation with the idea of "glory" in 2 Corinthians 3 and 4. In 3:7–11 the word appears ten times and then six more times by the end of chapter 4. Recall that the boldest of all of Moses' prayers was when he asked, "Please, show me your glory" (Ex. 33:18). What Moses received in answer to his prayer was a marvelous revelation of all of God's goodness as he proclaimed to him his name, the LORD. But Moses could not behold God's glory. He could see God's back but not his face (33:18–23). In the context of Exodus and the Old Testament revelation, this meant that no human could ever actually see the very essence of God's being. But God also withheld showing Moses his glory as a witness to a greater fulfillment yet to come. And it is that fulfillment Paul has in mind as he compares the glory with which the old covenant came—and it certainly was glorious—with the "glory that surpasses it" of "what is permanent" (2 Cor. 3:10–11).

And what is this surpassing (super-abounding, excellent) glory? For one thing, it is the fact that the power behind the new covenant is the Holy Spirit rather than written laws (3:6–8, 17; see also Ezek. 36:26–27). But there was more. Paul wanted his readers, then and now, to focus their attention on the person of Jesus Christ. The language of this passage makes it clear that in Jesus Christ we can know what Moses was unable to see, even though he sought it passionately. The idea of the veil shifts from a picture of the fading glory on the face of Moses to that which hides people from seeing the truth. "Only through Christ is it taken away. . . . When one turns to the Lord, the veil is removed" (3:14, 16). And what do we see when the veil is taken away? In Jesus, we, with unveiled faces, behold *the glory of the Lord* (3:18). The " glory of the Lord" resides in Jesus! Paul even uses the word *face* in the same way it was used in Exodus 33, where God's face was the same as his glory. We have "the light of the knowledge of the *glory* of God in the *face* of Jesus Christ" (4:6).

Familiar texts take on new depth of meaning with this perspective. "And the Word became flesh and dwelt among us, and we have seen his *glory, glory* as of the only Son from the Father, full of grace and truth" (John 1:14). Note the precise wording of Hebrews 1:3: "He is the *radiance* of the *glory of God.*" The word translated "radiance" here in the ESV has various translations in other versions, but the idea is always that of something bright and visible. In the coming of Jesus, that which has been invisible now can be seen. The word *radiance* also brings us back to the radiance on the face of Moses. Not only was it a "radiance [that] was fading away" (2 Cor. 3:13 NIV), but also it was only a *reflection* of the glory of God—Jesus' radiance is that very glory.

> Brightness of my Father's glory, Sunshine of my Father's face,
> Keep me ever trusting, resting; fill me with thy grace.
> Jesus, I am resting, resting, in the joy of what thou art;
> I am finding out the greatness of thy loving heart.

—JEAN SOPHIA PIGOTT (1876)

DAY 38

The Transforming Vision

2 Corinthians 3:18–4:6

> And we all, with unveiled face, beholding the glory of the Lord,
> are being transformed into the same image from one degree
> of glory to another. For this comes from the Lord who is the
> Spirit. . . . And even if our gospel is veiled, it is veiled only to
> those who are perishing. In their case the god of this world has
> blinded the minds of the unbelievers, to keep them from seeing
> the light of the gospel of the glory of Christ, who is the image
> of God. . . . For God, who said, "Let light shine out of darkness,"
> has shone in our hearts to give the light of the knowledge of the
> glory of God in the face of Jesus Christ. (2 Cor. 3:18; 4:3–4, 6)

Once it is understood that Jesus is the ultimate revelation of God's glory, we then need to consider *how* we are actually transformed so as to partake in that glory. That is the teaching of 2 Corinthians 3:18. Note that the verse speaks of a process that is presently going on in the life of a believer, and not the final, eternal glory that appears later in the passage (4:17). We "*are being* transformed into the same image from one degree of glory to another" (lit., "from glory to glory"). The word *transformed* comes directly from the Greek into English as *metamorphosis*, the process by which a caterpillar or other creature is changed from within to be radically altered in character and appearance. It is the same word that appears in Romans 12:2 where Paul exhorts, "Do not be conformed to this world, but be transformed by the renewal of your mind."

Paul tells just how this transformation will take place. It happens as we behold, as in a mirror, the glory of the Lord. (The word translated "behold" in the ESV or "reflect" in the NIV conveys only parts of this idea.) Visualize the common experience of looking into a mirror in such a way that you are able to see someone who is behind you or off to the side. We say that we see the person, when, in the most literal sense, what we are seeing is a reflection. Like Moses or any other mortal, we cannot directly view the glory of God. We do see, however, an exact reflection of that glory when we see Jesus.

The actual mirror through which we see the glory of God in Jesus is the gospel. In 2 Corinthians 4:4, Paul returns to the imagery of the veil to explain that if the gospel is veiled, it is because "the god of this world has blinded the minds [veiled the eyes] of the unbelievers, to keep them from seeing the light of the gospel of the glory of Christ, who is the image of God." The removal of the veil—our spiritual blindness—was not an act of our wills, but a supernatural work of God. As he says in 4:6, the very same power that created light in the first place brought light to our souls. In the beginning God said, "'Let there be light,' and there was light" (Gen. 1:3)—the word of creation. And God now says, "Let there be life, and there is life"—the word of the *new* creation!

Reread 4:6 thoughtfully and linger over every word, for it is an explanation of what the Lord did when he took away the veil. Because of God's regenerating power, we came to understand the gospel, and in believing it we were brought into "the light of the knowledge of the glory of God in the face of Jesus Christ." What Paul wants us to realize is that if we will look closely at the gospel, what we see is not only the message of sins forgiven, but a mirror in which we see Jesus. And in the face of Jesus, we have the knowledge of the glory of God. It was the gracious work of God that opened the gospel to us. That same grace, working through the power of the Holy Spirit (it "comes from the Lord who is the Spirit" [3:18]), is causing us to be transformed into the image of the Jesus we discovered in the gospel.

All the themes that we have been considering converge at this point: Moses' (and Paul's) passion to know God, his prayer to see God's glory, the revelation of God's name, the assurance of God's presence, God's gift of rest, and the radiance of Moses' face. All of these find fulfillment in Jesus. And as we behold this glory found in Jesus, we are "being transformed into the same image." We are being made to be like Christ one step at a time—"from one degree of glory to another" ("with an ever-increasing glory" NIV). Moses was only able to anticipate God's glory; we actually partake of it through the work of the Spirit within.

We struggle with the idea that our primary responsibility in this transforming process (usually defined as *sanctification*) is to fix our minds and hearts on Jesus. Our instinct is to look for something to do, some set of rules to follow. But to lapse into that kind of thinking would deny not only the teaching of this passage but also virtually every other teaching about sanctification in the New Testament. Romans 12:2, referred to earlier, says that we are to be transformed "by the renewal of your mind." The chapter in Colossians on the practical outworking of the Christian life begins, "If then you have been raised with Christ, seek the things that are above, where Christ is. . . . For you have died, and your life is hidden with Christ in God" (Col. 3:1, 3). There are very specific dos and don'ts that follow, and they are very important to the Christian life, but the basis of the new behavior is a focus on the exalted Christ. This is consistent with our study of prayers for the "knowledge of God." Out of the *knowing*—the heart set on Jesus—will come the *doing*. Peter said, "His divine power has granted to us all things that pertain to life and godliness, *through the knowledge of him* who called us to his own glory and excellence" (2 Peter 1:3).

Moses "endured as *seeing* him who is invisible" (Heb. 11:27). That same vision sustained Paul, and it will be more than sufficient for us as well.

Thou hast bid me gaze upon Thee, and Thy beauty fills my soul,
For by Thy transforming power, Thou hast made me whole.
Jesus, I am resting, resting, in the joy of what Thou art;
I am finding out the greatness of Thy loving heart.

—JEAN SOPHIA PIGOTT (1876)

DAY 39

Present Weakness

2 Corinthians 4:7–18

But we have this treasure in jars of clay, to show that the surpassing power belongs to God and not to us. We are afflicted
in every way, but not crushed; perplexed, but not driven to
despair; persecuted, but not forsaken; struck down, but not
destroyed; always carrying in the body the death of Jesus, so
that the life of Jesus may also be manifested in our bodies. . . .
For this light momentary affliction is preparing for us an eternal
weight of glory beyond all comparison, as we look not to the
things that are seen but to the things that are unseen. For the
things that are seen are transient, but the things that are unseen
are eternal. (2 Cor. 4:7–10, 17–18)

After filling our minds with thoughts of partaking of the divine
glory and being transformed into the very likeness of Christ
(3:18), the apostle Paul makes it clear that this is going on in the
midst of real life. We must not isolate this wonderful teaching
from our daily experience.

Paul reminds us that we are fragile beings—"jars of clay." Paul
certainly had in mind both the physical weakness of our mortal

bodies and the weakness of our flesh—that part of our being that relentlessly pulls us toward pride and selfishness. We are in these clay pots and will be until we go to be with Christ. Paul was resigned to this, and he said that it is supposed to be this way "to show that the surpassing power belongs to God and not to us" (4:7). Paul could even rejoice in his "thorn in the flesh" (12:7) so that he could know more about the sufficiency of God's grace. "Therefore I will boast all the more gladly of my weaknesses, so that the power of Christ may rest upon me" (12:9). Since Paul never disclosed just what this "thorn" was, we should feel free to insert our own "thorn" into our reading of that verse as we apply these truths to our lives.

In addition to the matter of human frailty, the apostle also had in mind the outward circumstances of life (2 Cor. 4:8–10; see also 6:3–10; 11:21–28). Life was not fair to Paul. In clear terms he told the Corinthians that he was afflicted in every way, perplexed, persecuted, and struck down. In addition to other hardships Paul experienced in his service for Christ, it appears from the way he wrote that he was criticized for being willing to endure those hardships in the first place (3:1–2; 11:16–20). It seems that the Corinthians were looking for evidence that following Christ leads only to the good life. Paul's difficulties, they reasoned, were surely his own fault. Most of us entertain the same kinds of thoughts when we try to explain our difficulties or those of others. "What is wrong with me [or them]?" we ask. But Paul saw no need to "lose heart" (4:1, 16), and he could look beyond his weaknesses and circumstances because he possessed a treasure.

The context makes it clear what Paul meant by "this treasure" (4:7). Through the Spirit of the Lord, the veil had been taken away and he was liberated (3:16–17). He was liberated from his earthbound perspective on life and could, therefore, see Jesus, the risen and exalted Lord (4:13–14). Paul knew that he was already partaking of "the glory of God in the face of Jesus" (4:6; see also 3:18). This was his treasure. Therefore, Paul saw no need to lose heart, because living meant ministry and the sharing of his treasure with more and more people (4:5, 15).

In the concluding meditation we will consider the final and eternal glory. But first recognize that our treasure, like Paul's, is more than sufficient for *this* life as well. I believe there has been a serious misrepresentation of biblical teaching in the common idea that our treasure is merely a home in heaven, so we endure this life and its troubles by dwelling on thoughts of heaven. Since few of us really live this way, we struggle with our lack of spirituality. But, in fact, our treasure is Jesus! We can live this life with joy and purpose because it is a course that he has laid out for us. Our "light momentary affliction" (4:17) is of no real consequence, for when we look past it, we see Jesus.

The privilege of living for Jesus in even the most difficult circumstances is summarized beautifully in Hebrews 12:

> Therefore, since we are surrounded by so great a cloud of witnesses [Moses and all the other heroes of faith named in chap. 11], let us also lay aside every weight, and sin which clings so closely, and let us run with endurance the race that is set before us, looking to Jesus, the founder and perfecter of our faith, who for the joy that was set before him endured the cross, despising the shame, and is seated at the right hand of the throne of God. Consider him who endured from sinners such hostility against himself, so that you may not grow weary or fainthearted. (Heb. 12:1–3)

DAY 40

Eternal Glory

2 Corinthians 4:16–18; Colossians 3:1–4

> If then you have been raised with Christ, seek the things that
> are above, where Christ is, seated at the right hand of God. Set
> your minds on things that are above, not on things that are on
> earth. For you have died, and your life is hidden with Christ in
> God. When Christ who is your life appears, then you also will
> appear with him in glory. (Col. 3:1–4)

Our "forty days on the mountain" will conclude with more
thoughts about glory. Moses prayed to see the glory of God and was
allowed to come close enough to see the Lord's back but not his
face. In our day of the new covenant, through the ministry of the
Spirit, we see "the glory of God in the face of Jesus Christ" (2 Cor.
4:6). But it is a poor reflection—a dim mirror (1 Cor. 13:12)—because
of the distortions of our flesh. However, if even that reflection
is transforming us "into his likeness with ever increasing glory"
(2 Cor. 3:18 NIV), imagine what it will be like when we are present
with Christ in the fullness of his majesty and glory!

It is the anticipation of that greater glory that animated the
faith and life of the apostle Paul, and it should do the same for us.

"So we do not lose heart," he said to the Corinthians (4:16). The deterioration of the outward man is unimportant, and his light momentary affliction is only a stepping-stone to eternal glory. This could be a reality because he did not look "to the things that are seen but to the things that are unseen" (4:18). The unseen, which is eternal, is the risen and exalted Christ along with the anticipation of being with him for eternity.

Notice that Paul's thoughts in Colossians 3 parallel those of 2 Corinthians 4. We are to set our hearts and minds on "the things that are above, where Christ is, seated at the right hand of God" (Col. 3:1). That doesn't mean we are to think solely about what is waiting for us in "heaven," but to focus on Christ himself in his exaltation. That is where the most essential part of our being is hidden. In the future there will come a time when "Christ who is [our] life" (3:4) will appear, and then we will appear with him and share in his glory. The entire discussion of the Christian life that follows (Col. 3:5–4:1) builds on this fundamental perspective on life.

These texts challenge the common perception of defining life as simply waiting to go to heaven. Personally, I have to be honest and say that such a definition of life is not a strong motivator for me to follow Christ. I'm sure it reflects something of my earth-bound vision, but I hope it also reflects a desire to be faithful to biblical teaching. When Paul and other New Testament authors speak of heaven or things above or what is unseen, the terms refer essentially to the presence of Christ at the right hand of the Father. Focusing on heaven in that sense *is* tremendously satisfying. Furthermore, the anticipation of actually being in that presence, with all barriers removed, is a very exciting prospect—whether it comes as a consequence of death or at the day of Christ's return.

The late C. S. Lewis had a very Christ-centered perspective of heaven, and he moves our imagination to see more of the future glory before us. The following are a series of quotations taken from his sermon, "The Weight of Glory," delivered in 1941. In the earlier part of the sermon Lewis wrestled with the question of the worthiness of longing for heaven. But then he reviews the biblical promises and reflects on the meaning of glory.

> At present we are on the outside of the world, the wrong side of the door. We discern the freshness and purity of the morning, but they do not make us fresh and pure. We cannot mingle with the splendors we see. But all the leaves of the New Testament are rustling with the rumor that it will not always be so. Some day, God willing, we shall get in. . . . We are summoned to pass in through Nature, beyond her, into that splendor which she fitfully reflects.
>
> And in there, in beyond Nature, we shall eat of the tree of life. At present, if we are reborn in Christ, the spirit in us lives directly on God; but the mind and, still more, the body receives life from Him at a thousand removes. . . . What would it be to taste at the fountainhead that stream of which even these lower reaches prove so intoxicating? Yet that, I believe, is what lies before us. The whole man is to drink joy at the fountain of joy. . . .
>
> Meanwhile the cross comes before the crown and tomorrow is a Monday morning. A cleft has opened in the pitiless walls of the world, and we are invited to follow our great Captain inside. The following Him is, of course, the essential point.[1]

1. C. S. Lewis, *The Weight of Glory and Other Addresses* (San Francisco: HarperCollins, 2001), 39–45.

The Next Forty Days

It is my prayer that after reading through *Forty Days on the Mountain* you have a new desire to grow in your knowledge of God. Moses' encounter with the Lord is a doorway we can step through onto a path of discovery, but the path of knowing more of God is one we will be following for the rest of our lives. Here are a few thoughts about specific steps you could take as you go through the doorway.

The most important step is to continue (or perhaps begin) a consistent reading of the Bible itself. Set a schedule for yourself or make use of the many published helps that are available. Crossway offers the reading plan of Robert Murray M'Cheyne in outline form as well as the two-volume guide to M'Cheyne's plan by D. A. Carson, *For the Love of God*. I also recommend the material of Scripture Union in Valley Forge, Pennsylvania, called *Encounter with God*. It is a daily, guided Scripture reading that includes a brief meditation on the passage for the day, similar to the format that I followed.

It is important that we appreciate the value of our hymnals as aids in devotion, including the Bible's own hymnal, the book of Psalms. I try to actually sing or say the psalms or hymns quietly rather than just read them. For me at least, this seems to engage my attention to a greater degree.

Reading *Forty Days* is an introduction to Christian spirituality. It is tragic that in our frantic culture, many overlook the wonderful treasure house in the writings of men and women who have sought to enter more deeply into the knowledge of God. What follows are suggestions for further reading by those authors who have been helpful to me. I offer this list with the understanding that those who have been helpful to me will not necessarily have the same impact on you.

I first of all highly recommend the writing of A. W. Tozer. The book I quoted in the meditations, *The Pursuit of God*, is a book of extraordinary depth, and I never find it stale with repeated readings. I profited recently from Tozer's *The Knowledge of the Holy*, a series of meditations on the attributes of God.

For more substantial books to strengthen your understanding of God, I recommend *Knowing God* by J. I. Packer. This is not a devotional reading, but the investment in reading will be very rewarding. You should also become acquainted with the excellent work of John Piper. He will teach you about "Christian hedonism"—finding the highest possible joy through seeking God.

It should be apparent from your reading of the meditations that I appreciate the writing of the late Henri Nouwen. I have found him refreshing because he writes from the perspective of a different tradition—that of Roman Catholicism. But that difference will also necessitate caution about some of his views. Most of his writings (such as *Road from Daybreak*) are published journals. I have particularly enjoyed this form of writing because it can be read in small bites.

Finally, keep in mind that coming to know God is not just a personal quest. If we are to grow, we must be hearing the Scripture preached and experiencing the fellowship of the saints in a healthy church. Spiritual maturity comes about as "we all attain to the unity of the faith and of the knowledge of the Son of God.... We are to grow up in every way into him who is the head, into Christ" (Eph. 4:13, 15).